BRYLCREEM AND BROKEN BISCUITS

A Street Trail History of Bradford on Avon's Shops in the 1950s

Cover: Market Street in the early 1950s

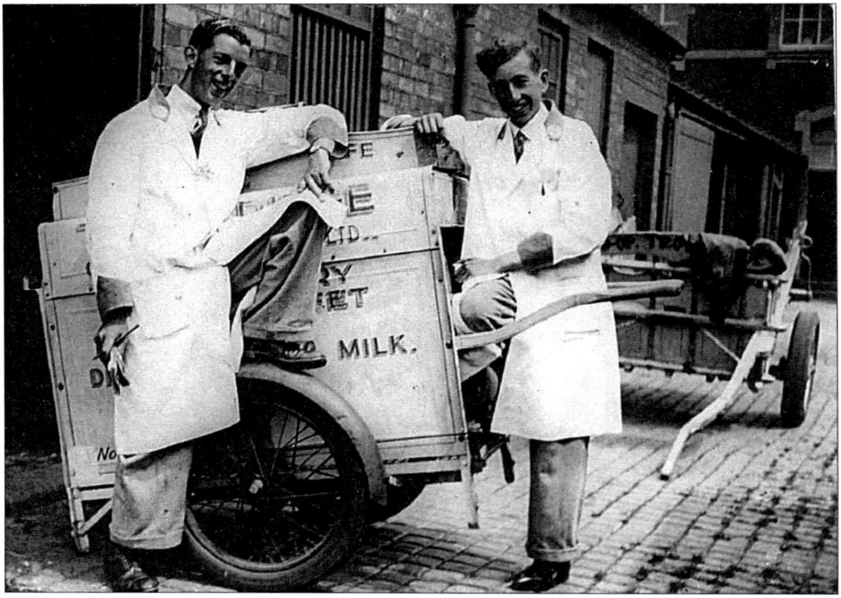

Daily dairy deliveries, Bradford on Avon, c. 1950

Brylcreem

and

Broken Biscuits

~

A Street Trail History of Bradford on Avon's shops in the 1950s

~

Stephanie Laslett

Ex Libris Press

Published in 2013
and reprinted in 2020 by
EX LIBRIS PRESS
11 Regents Place
Bradford on Avon
Wiltshire BA15 1ED

Origination by Ex Libris Press

www.ex-librisbooks.co.uk

ISBN 978-1-906641-57-3

CONTENTS

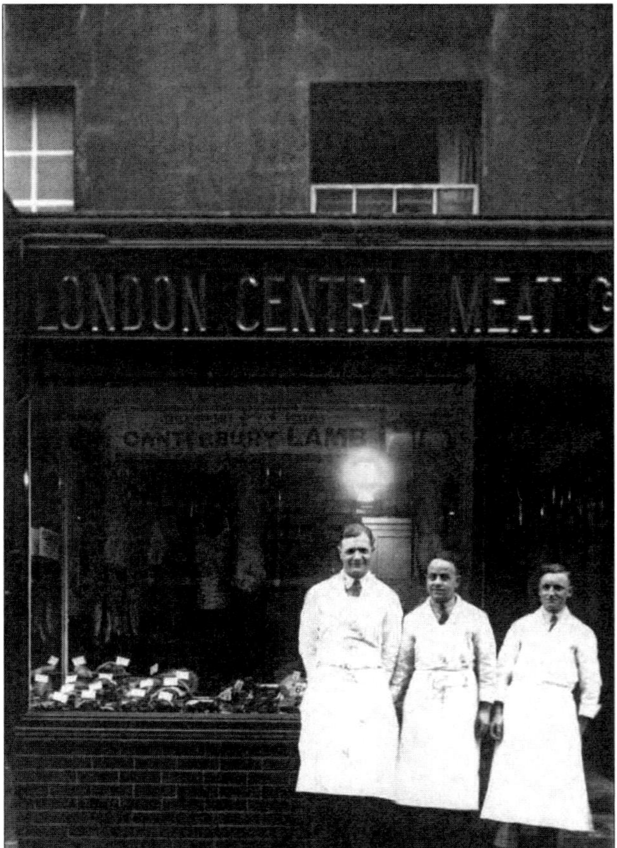

The London Central Meat Company, No 2 The Shambles, c. 1911

Preface

Although we moved to the Limpley Stoke valley in 1990, I've lived in the centre of Bradford on Avon only since 2010, hardly long enough to feel qualified to write about the place. But in 2012, in response to the Town Council's request for ideas on how to celebrate the Queen's Diamond Jubilee, I suggested it would be interesting to look at what the shops were like back in 1952. The local shopkeepers were very supportive and in June every shop window in the town centre had an exhibition panel with details of what had been there sixty years previously, with photographs I'd sourced from the Bradford on Avon Museum, the Wiltshire and Swindon History Centre, Neil Mattingley of www.freshford.com and local people – and texts I'd compiled with the help of local residents who had very generously agreed to share their memories with me through recorded conversations.

Roger Jones of Ex Libris Press saw the material and thought it might be worth compiling in a more permanent form, hence this book.

The recorded reminiscences form part of the Bradford Hundred Memory Bank established by Margaret Dobson from recordings she began in 1989. To identify the contributors I have repeated the convention of initials and the year of interview she used in her fascinating book *Bradford Voices* which contains much more material covering all aspects of life in the town since 1900. Margaret has kindly given me permission to include several quotes from her book, for which I am most grateful.

The area covered by this book is limited to the centre of town: Market Street, Church Street, The Shambles, Silver Street, Bridge Street and St Margaret's Street. Identifying the shops from old street directories proved a challenge, not least because the numbers switched from the anti-clockwise system introduced in 1884 to a clockwise direction in 1904. Prior to 1884 there was no numbering at all.

I have tried to focus on the shops and the 1950s, but occasionally have strayed into more general 'trade' territory – and have gone further back in time to provide a fuller picture. The photographs are all from the 1950s unless otherwise captioned. Many items from Bradford's old shops can be seen in Bradford on Avon Museum on the top floor of the Library building in Bridge Street.

My thanks to the residents of Bradford on Avon for sharing their memories, to the shopkeepers of Bradford on Avon, Bradford on Avon Museum (and particularly Roger Clark for his encyclopaedic knowledge of the town and the excellent website www.bradfordonavonmuseum.co.uk), Bradford on Avon Town Council, Bradford on Avon Chamber of Commerce (and particularly Caroline Philpott), Mike Marshman and the staff at the Wiltshire & Swindon History Centre, Neil Mattingley of the wonderful website www.freshford.com, the Bradford Hundred Memory Bank team (and particularly Margaret Dobson for her help and generosity and Liz Corfield for transcribing the memories), Gareth Slater for his map, Sam Illingworth for testing the route, Christian Penny, Colin Johns, Louise Gummer, Roger Mawby and, finally, Arlene Caddow and Mark Kendall of Fat Fowl for generously sponsoring the book.

If you have photographs or memories of life in Bradford on Avon, the Bradford on AvonMuseum and the Bradford Hundred Memory Bank would love to hear from you. Please contact them via mervyn@mervynharris26.plus.com 01225-863440.

As was the case in the 1950s, we are still very fortunate in this little town to enjoy the quality, quantity and variety of our excellent small shops, run by friendly and knowledgeable shopkeepers, and a bustling weekly market. Long may they all continue to thrive!

Stephanie Laslett
Bradford on Avon
June 2013

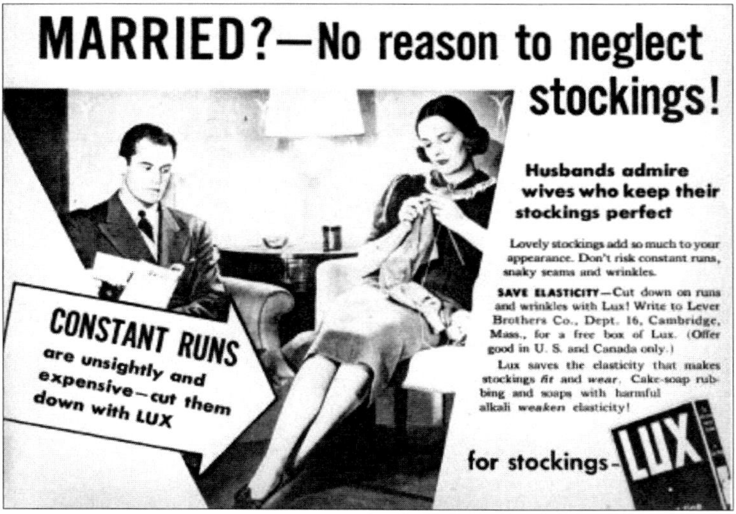

Introduction

Trade and shopkeeping in Bradford on Avon

Although this book focuses on Bradford on Avon's shops in 1952, it is interesting to look at how trade and shopkeeping developed within the town from its earliest days, particularly during the 18th and 19th centuries when the town's fortunes were so closely tied to the local cloth industry. Throughout much of its history, as with other small towns, Bradford was almost entirely self-sufficient. Local produce and cattle were sold at the market and travelling pedlars provided the only glimpse of exotic goods from 'foreign' parts, such as Bristol.

From its foundation as an Iron Age settlement on Budbury, the earliest form of trade would have been the exchange of cattle and goods for coins, continuing through Roman, Saxon and Norman times. It's likely that a regular market took place in the town during Saxon times but the earliest written reference is in the Domesday Book of 1086 when it was recorded as part of the Abbess of Shaftesbury's manorial holdings and valued at 45 shillings.[1] Canon William H. Jones, the vicar of Holy Trinity Church and esteemed local historian writing in the late Victorian period, calculated that the population of the town would have been about three to four hundred at the time.[2] When John Leland visited the town in 1540 he noted a "good market once a week".[3]

By around 1300 Bradford had set itself up in the cloth trade. By the mid-14th century the industry was thriving and, with some ups and downs, would still be going strong some five hundred years later. From the 14th century accounts of the Abbess of Shaftesbury's manor we know that at the far end of Church Street there were four shops, along with manorial barns and a pigeon house by the gate of the lay courthouse. In 1372 there were 14 market stalls, most likely in the old market place in Silver Street and by 1392 there were five shops in Fox Street, later renamed Silver Street.[4]

The buildings along the south side of The Shambles date from around 1400 when this would have been the heart of the town, much as it is today. The old market place at the Silver Street end of the Shambles housed the pillory and whipping post and was possibly the site of the horrific fate suffered by Thomas Traynell in 1532 or thereabouts, when he was burnt at the stake for heresy.[5]

Bradford's cloth industry dominated the town throughout this time, but by the second half of the 18th century, with strong competition from the Yorkshire woollen mills and a preference for lighter weight cloth, Bradford was struggling. The rising price of food added to the hardship experienced during these testing times. Wages were reduced, food prices rocketed and people were hungry and desperate. Punishment was harsh for those who took risks to feed their families. In 1766 a Bradford broadweaver was hanged for stealing bacon. Harold Fassnidge, in his book *Bradford on Avon: Past and Present*, calculated that in 1785 a labourer's 12-hour day would earn him just enough to buy a small loaf of bread and some butter – hardly enough to feed himself let alone his children. The threat to jobs posed by new technology led to the 1791 riots in St Margaret's Street when a scribbling horse, a new invention for carding wool, was burned on the bridge and three people within the rebellious mob were shot to death by Mr Phelps the clothier outside his home, Westbury House, in the centre of town.

These hard times saw the foundation of one of Bradford's most successful and enduring grocers, at 33 Silver Street. The Budgett family started their business in 1775 and by 1871 had expanded into the shop next door. By 1897 they had diversified and were selling chinaware – and even renting out horses and carriages – until finally shutting up shop in 1899. In the 1950s, the period of the Street Trail forming the bulk of this book, the shop was once again a grocers, run by the highly successful Bradford on Avon Co-operative Society.

This period also saw the emergence of town directories listing local notables such as gentry and clergy, and the trades of the time. The *Universal British Directory* covered the years 1793 to 1798. Curiously, despite the evident poverty in the town, the directory proudly claimed that provisions from the Bradford area were so abundant that surplus produce was sent up to London by river.

In 1793 the directory lists six bakers, six grocers and three butchers in the centre of town. Despite the hardship experienced by many, the wealthy clothiers would not have experienced much suffering. The town had ten businesses related to clothing apparel and there was evidently sufficient demand to support two peruke or wig makers.

Trade would have been largely confined to local goods throughout this time. Two goods carriers operated coaches twice a week from London to Bath in 1740 – but Bath was very different to Bradford on Avon. By 1822 a 'handsome and commodious wharf' on the Kennet and Avon Canal at Bradford on Avon was handling 'considerable trade' from London and by 1841 the main goods carriers, Hillier & May's, were operating wagons three times a week, leaving the Queen's Head in Bridge Street (which occupied the right-hand side of The Three Gables), for Trowbridge and London.[6] Benjamin Bolwell operated a boat between Canal Wharf and Bath and Bristol twice a week, taking two days to get there.[7]

Goods were traded in the weekly market in Silver Street which in 1792 was on a Monday, but by 1822 had moved to Saturday.[8] A corn and cattle market took place every other Tuesday. Small rings, still to be seen on the west wall of the town bridge, are said to date from this time, when beasts were tethered ready for sale.[9] By 1841 the market had moved to Pippet Street, now renamed Market Street.

By 1820 the cloth industry had been in serious decline for some years with disastrous consequences for the workers. It is shocking to discover that a report to the Home Secretary in 1821 recorded four suicides in a single day – in Bradford on Avon alone.[10]

Food prices continued to spark conflict. A riot kicked off on a May market day in 1826 when the price of potatoes went up from 5d to 6d a peck. A market gardener was almost killed before the mob turned on the butchers. The ringleader was thrown into the lock up on the bridge but, astonishingly – and alarmingly, given its precarious situation overhanging the river - the incensed crowd tore the roof off in order to free him.[11]

The 1830s seem to have been a more prosperous decade altogether. The trade directories showed an increase in certain trades: butchers almost doubled between 1830 and 1842, as did boot and shoemakers.[12] The number of grocers rocketed from nine in 1830 to 28 in 1842. Gee Langdon in her engrossing book *The Year of the Map*, describing Bradford life in 1841, notes that there were shoemakers on every street, with nine on Whitehill alone.[13]

These were lively times for the traders. The streets would have rung with their cries, as colourfully described by a resident at that time, Daniel Batchelor, who emigrated to New York in the late 19th century and wrote a long letter to the *North Wiltshire Mercury* in 1885 with reminiscences of life in Bradford in the 1830s:

> "Old Molly Dix who used to sell saloop[14] or sloop on Bradford Bridge more than fifty years ago, was able to hold her own against all comers, ostler or jarvies[15], in the rougher specimens of Saxon. Jim Whittaker the watercress man was highly accomplished in the primitive local speech. But of all the voices that rang through the air in the old town that of Becky's who sold hot cakes, was the shrillest. She would lift up her staccato of hot cakes in such ear piercing tones as could be heard from Bradford Bridge to Budbury Hill. What has become of the donkey drivers who used to bring their animals laden with sacks of coals to the Bullpit? The sand pedlar too, perhaps he does not now stop at the Old Bear door [still there in Silver Street]and urge the Land lady with such persuasions 'Naow Missus 'tes a good bag o zand an ya'd better t'yak an ya'n,' &c. Does the town crier yet announce in season that you can buy "fine fresh mackerel at the Old Bear door?" [16]

But this was probably the boom before the bust. The failure of the local bank in 1841 led to yet more misery which, as Canon Jones wrote, "cast an abiding gloom over the town." Four hundred people were moved into the poorhouse at Avoncliff, barely able to hold a fraction of that number. With no sign of employment in the offing, workers and their families left the town in droves. Bradford's population was reduced, according to Canon Jones' calculations, by about a quarter in the ten years between 1841 and 1851, decreasing from 6,781 to 5,331.[17]

The first mention of hairdressers in Bradford's commercial directories is seen in 1842, at a time when the town was really suffering. It's tempting to find a parallel with the phenomenon seen during our current economic crisis, with people turning to "cheap" luxuries such as nail bars to lift the spirits. However, the reality was that the hairdressers would have been used almost exclusively by the local gentry and clothing magnates.

In 1848 we see the first directory entries for two patten and clogmakers, in Silver Street and New Market Place (now part of Market Street). Again, it's tempting to link this to the launch of the new industry started in the town in that same year when Stephen Moulton opened one of England's first rubber works in Kingston Mill. But clogs and pattens would have been widely worn prior to this and their inclusion probably reflects the publisher's determination to get every trade and shop in his directory.

These directories featured wonderfully ornate advertisements testing the trust of even the most gullible. In the 1869 *Rawling's Directory* an advert for 'Dr Locock's Pulmonic Wafers' guarantees 'Perfect freedom from coughs in ten minutes' and 'Rapid Cure of...all disorders of the breath and lungs'. Adverts frequently took the form of messages of thanks to loyal customers:

> "Ledbury & Sons, Practical Tailors, Habit and Breeches Makers of Pipet [sic] Street, tender their most sincere thanks for the kind support they have received and they trust by producing garments of the most approved style of fashion and by diligence and punctuality . . to obtain a continuance of the same."

In the same directory the drapers, Jennings, "thanks the public for the kind support he has already received, and hopes by selling goods at the smallest shade of remunerating profit, to ensure a large increase thereof." A far cry from "PRICES SLASHED!!!!"

The 1886 directory shows Mr England of the Shambles rather disconcertingly combining two roles: Rate Collector and Razor Strop Maker. At this time in the heart of the town there were ten boot and shoe makers, twelve drapers and outfitters, five bakers, five butchers and seven grocers all vying for trade. Shopkeepers relied on their window displays to attract customers, none more impressive than Seymours Butchers in Silver Street.

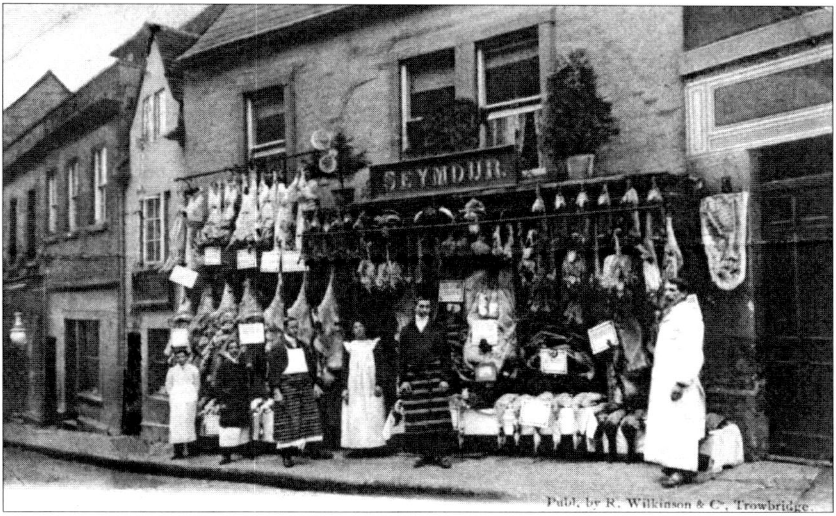

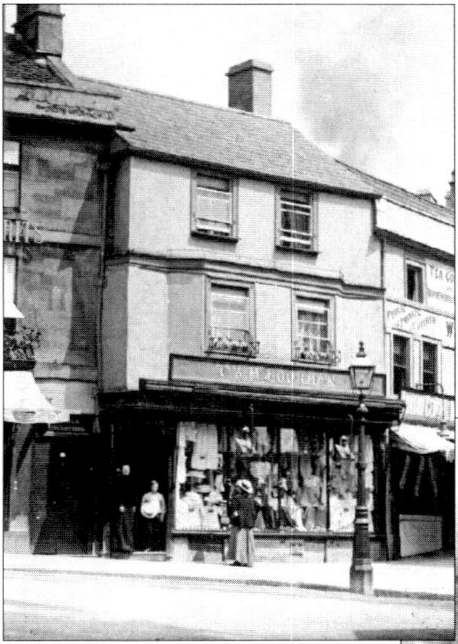

Above: Seymour's Butchers, 10 Silver Street, c. 1903

Left: Boorman's Drapers, 36 Market Street, c. 1903

Below: Couplands Grocers, 4 The Shambles, c. 1917

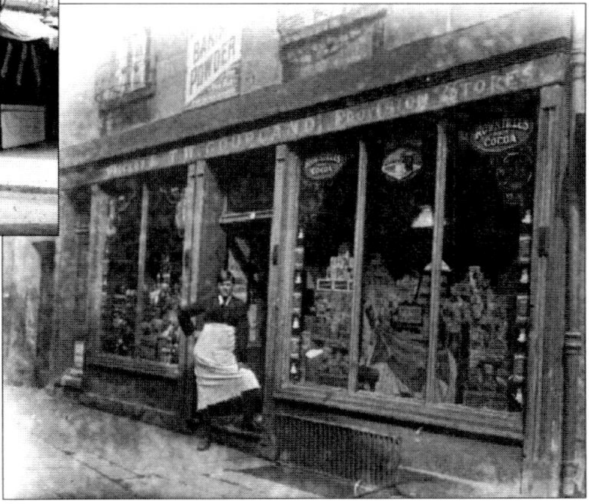

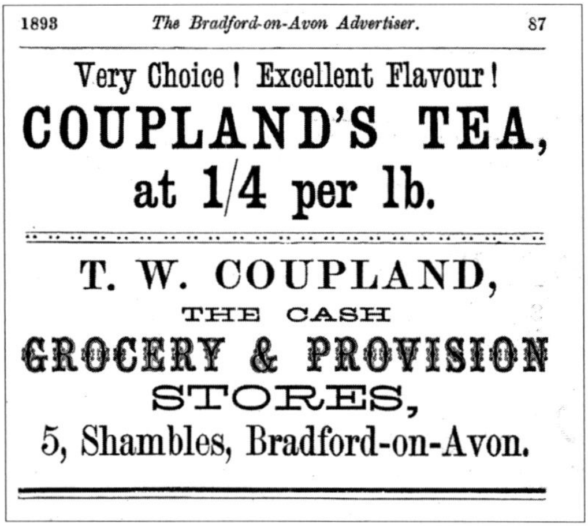

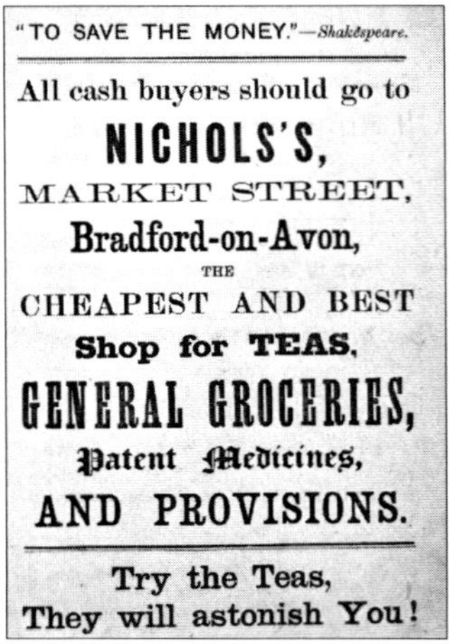

Stephen Moulton's new rubber industry helped revive Bradford's fortunes during this time but the population continued to decline, falling from 4,957 to 4,512 between 1891 and 1901.[18] Hard times continued for many right up until the beginning of the twentieth century when a soup kitchen was set up in Barton Orchard[19], in common with many other parts of the country.

Bradford's weekly market appears to have stopped abruptly in 1903 but today happily continues on a Thursday in the Library car park. The start of the 20th century also saw the emergence of two enduring businesses: Knee's Stores and the new Post Office on the site shown on page 16.

The First World War had a devastating impact on trade and prices throughout the UK – and on local businesses as men were called up for active service. Margaret Dobson's *Bradford Voices* gives a fascinating account of the applications for exemption made to the Bradford Tribunal, regularly printed in the local paper. Successful appeals included three months' exemption to Donald Keates, who ran a motor cycle business, one month to Jesse Dicks, a coal merchant, and exemption to Nelson Uncles, whose father ran an important iron foundry, considered vital from an agricultural standpoint. Sadly, Donald's three month exemption was not repeated and he was to die during the war, leaving his two brothers to continue the business. Bradford's three bakers were continually called before the Tribunal but their essential role in feeding the town ensured an exemption which continued throughout the war. Albert Dodge, the shoemaker in Silver Street (and still there in 1952), was not so lucky. Shoe prices had doubled since the start of the war and he pleaded his case on the basis that people were now reliant on continual shoe repairs, but to no avail.[20]

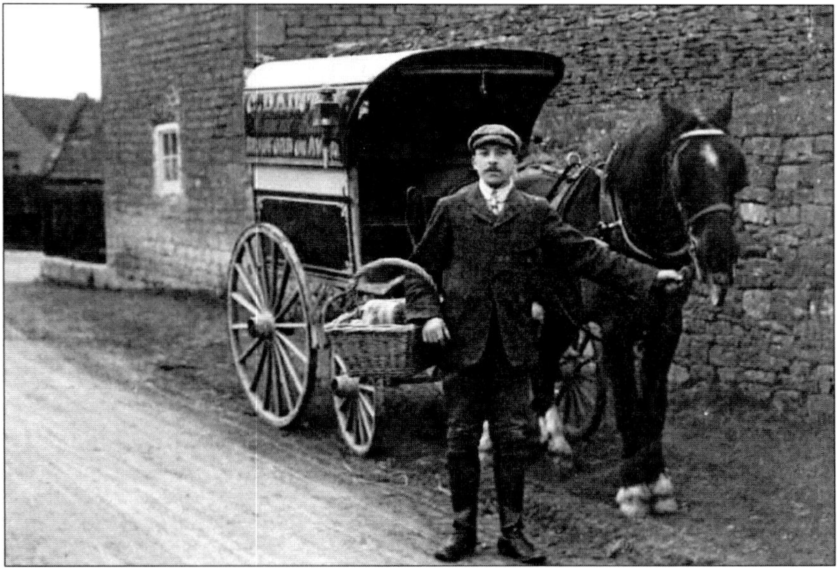

Frank Dainton with the bakery van, 1910

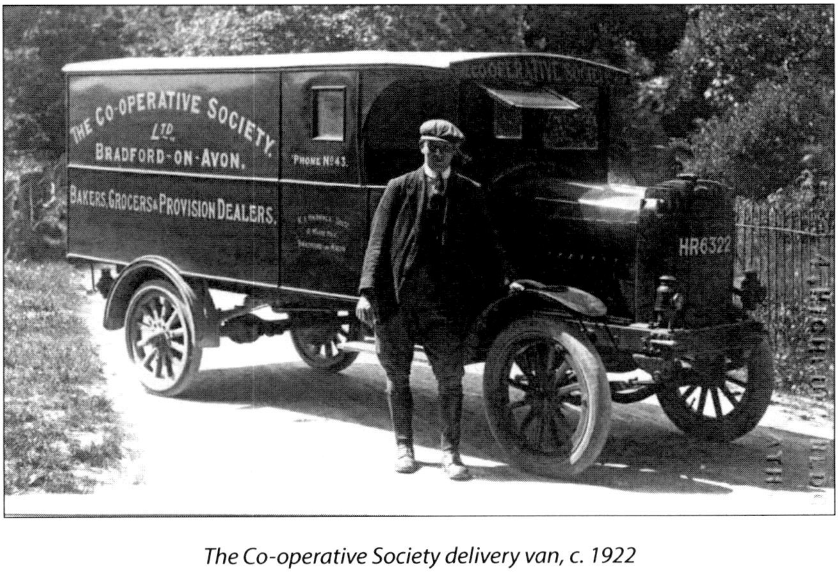

The Co-operative Society delivery van, c. 1922

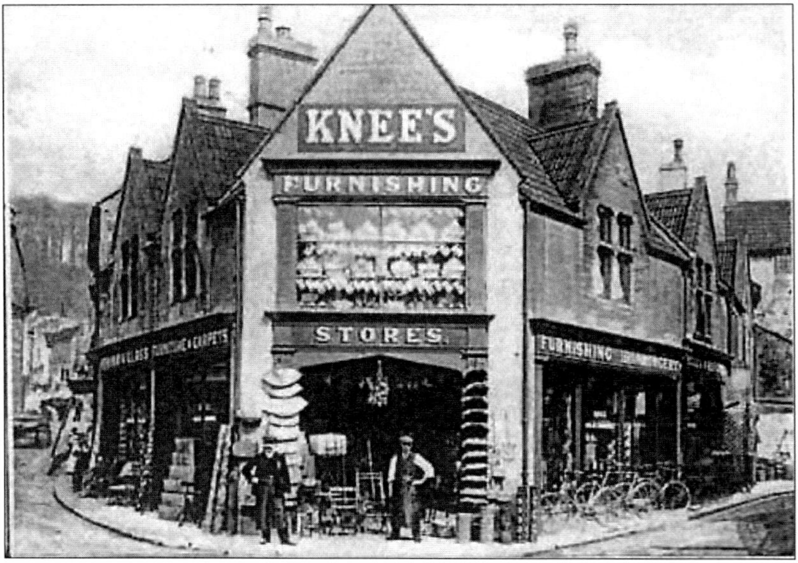

Knee's Store shortly after it opened in 1905 at the corner of Market Street and Silver Street, demolished in 1967

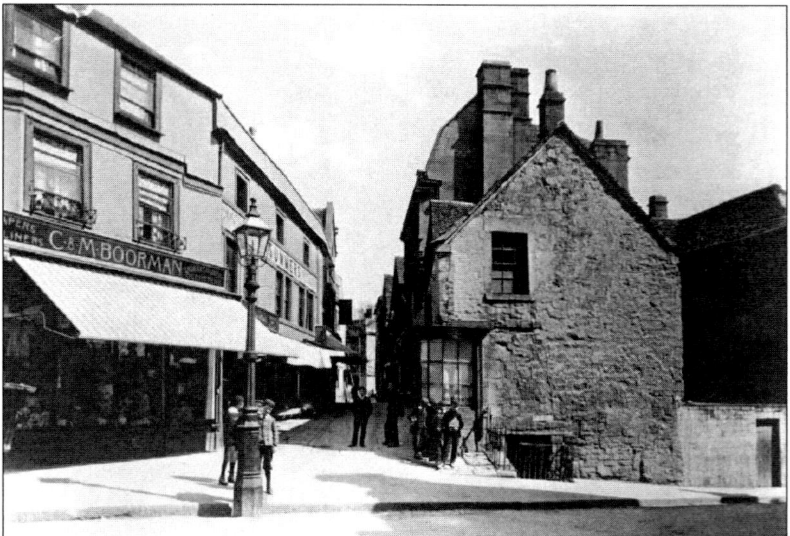

The old building on the south-west corner of The Shambles c. 1900, shortly before it was demolished to make way for the Post Office

Food rationing was put in place in 1917 and any local businesses found profiteering were swiftly punished. Even after the war was over, food prices reached their highest point for 25 years in 1925 and there were pockets of genuine poverty throughout the town. Local shops were struggling to pick up the pieces after the huge loss of life, but gradually businesses began to recover and even thrive. One of the best known in this period was Bryant's hardware store. Mr Bryant's horsedrawn cart, later replaced by a Model T Ford, carried a remarkable range of goods around Bradford and the outlying villages. This service continued into the 1950s.

The Second World War brought an influx of temporary settlers to Bradford on Avon, from American troops to East End mothers and babies, putting additional strain on the dwindling resources in the town. Rationing was introduced in 1940 to help eke out food supplies. Jack Mock gives a fascinating insight into this period in his account of the war years, also featured in *Bradford Voices*.[21]

More information about Bradford's retailers from the Victorian period up to the 1950s is given in the Street Trail section of this book under each individual shop.

The 1950s – forging modern Britain

After the deprivations of wartime, Britain was buoyed up by a new spirit of optimism, the birth rate was booming and a workforce home from the front, now swelled by large numbers of working women, was keen to meet the growing demand for goods and services. After a period of severe austerity, the 1950s was a decade when consumers were striving to improve their home comforts and standard of living. Housewives benefited from new technology and young people re-invented themselves as teenagers. A revolution in fashion and music was to pave the way for the liberal 1960s.

However, in 1952, the year on which this Street Trail focuses, the aftermath of war was still keenly felt as rationing continued, housewives queued and children played on open bomb sites. On 21st February 1952 Churchill abolished the personal identity card, a significant gesture which signalled a new confidence.

Despite many women taking up work during wartime, in the early Fifties it was still very much the norm for mothers to focus on being good housewives. Indeed, women's magazines of the time encouraged their readers to stay at home to rear the next generation and leave the workplace free for men to be in full employment after being demobbed from the forces. The average family had 3.5 children in 1952 compared to 1.7 now, with just 4% born out of wedlock, almost 50% now. Divorce back then was around 33,000 a year, about a quarter of the current figure.[22]

In 1951 a Mass Observation study discovered that Mrs Average Housewife was working a 75 hour week, a quarter of which was spent in the kitchen getting to grips with the startling convenience of fish fingers and teabags, both invented in the 1950s. Little wonder she greeted the new labour-saving gadgets so enthusiastically.[23] Mod cons such as the fridge were still very expensive, owned by around one family in twenty, and home freezers were unheard of at this time. The washtub and mangle were being replaced by the twin-tub washing machine and housewives were freed from the drudgery of Monday wash day.

Families were very home-oriented. Around a third were able to afford their own home, with the majority renting. After a long 42 hour week the average worker's leisure time was spent reading, listening to the radio (a select few had televisions in 1952), knitting, needlework and gardening. Children had freedom to play outdoors, or if cooped up inside, were busy building stamp collections. If lucky enough to have a television, they would have enjoyed *Bill and Ben, the Flowerpot Men*, launched in 1952. Later in the 1950s young people broke away from the convention of dressing exactly like their parents as they reached adulthood. With almost zero unemployment and a regular income there was a newfound confidence to walk away from conventional expectations and form their own sub-group. Not only were teenagers demanding new styles but new fabrics such as nylon and polyester emerged from the petrochemicals industry, leading to fresh approaches to colour and print. Brylcreem (and a comb always at the ready) and hairspray enabled the young to model elaborate hairstyles which further distinguished them from their parents.

Music played an equally large part in signalling this division. The development of the transistor radio in the 1950s led to portable and cheaper record players such as the Dansette, introduced in 1952 and small enough for young people to play in their own rooms away from the controlling influence of their parents. With the invention of vinyl and the first 33rpm "long-playing" record, the records themselves became affordable for the young. These technological breakthroughs coincided with a musical revolution. In 1952 musical tastes had not changed radically from the 1940s, but rock and roll was just around the corner. Fender produced the first mass produced solid body electric guitar, in 1954 Bill Haley released *Rock around the clock* and things were never the same again.

Change was in the air but the consumer age was still some way ahead. Shoppers were not bombarded by advertising in the way they are now. TV advertising was unknown before 1959 and magazine ads were rather quaint, although astonishingly sexist to our eyes, as seen on page 23. Cigarette ads also demonstrate how attitudes have changed. "Craven A completes the perfect understanding between young people together. Always kind to your throat. Craven A – the unanimous approval of the whole wide world."

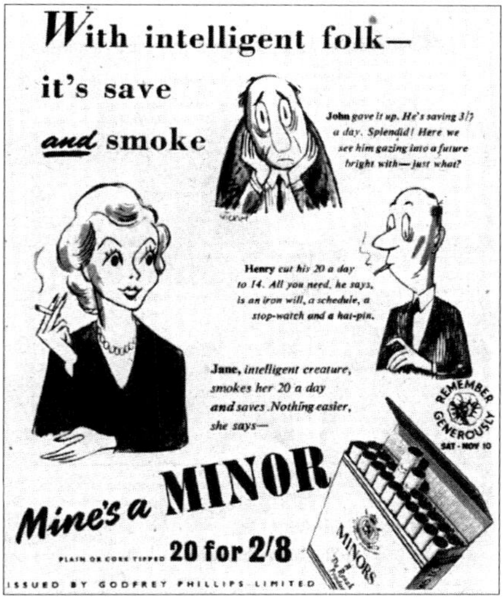

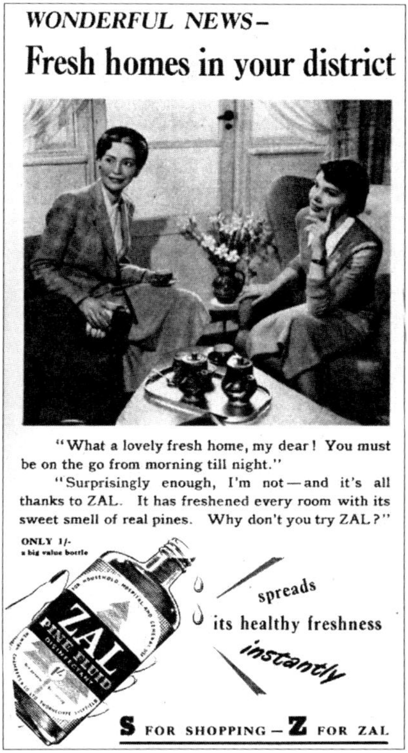

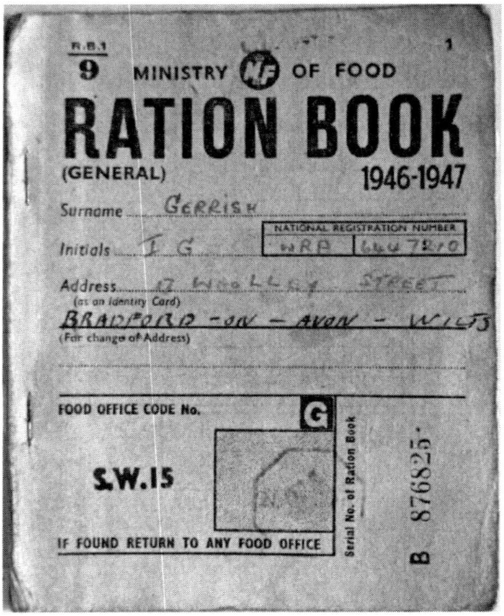

Mr I G Gerrish's ration book, supplied by the Ministry of Food

Bradford on Avon in the 1950s

Although structurally much the same as we see today, the centre of Bradford was a very different place in the 1950s to the town which attracts tourists today. Certain sections of Wine Street, Whitehill, Tory and Middle Rank, whilst not as notorious as they had been in the 1920s and '30s, were still pretty dilapidated and faced widespread demolition, successfully fought off in some cases. Spencer Moulton, later Avon Rubber, brought a degree of prosperity to the town but also had a wider impact on the look of the place. Buildings were blackened from years of factory chimney smoke and even the inhabitants wore their share of the output.

> *"We used to put the pram on the steps outside, and I always remember looking at Jeremy in the pram and there were tiny little black dots on his face, and I thought it was exhaust fumes, but in fact it was soot from the rubber factory."* (AJ11)

> *"Doctor wanted me out of the factory because you'd come out covered in chalk, you see. From the type of work there was in those days the rubber was always sticky and it had to be chalked, you know, and of course it would fly about and you'd come out with white hair. (It got into your lungs) and I had a bit of a skin problem."* (DP11)

Regrettably in some ways, local industry has diminished since those days but what about the shops? How different were they?

The town shops in the 1950s

For much of its life Bradford had been almost entirely self-sufficient and even in the Fifties people were able to get most of what they needed without ever leaving the town.

A local resident described the town in the Sixties, but it equally applied to the decade before:

> *"... what I found so amazing was that it was completely self-sufficient. It was a very small town but it had all the necessary shops. We had shoe shops, we had clothes shops, endless grocery shops, butchers, greengrocers. There was an electricity shop; all the amenity shops were here, which have mostly gone now. Not unnaturally, it had a great charm."* (VJ11)

In 1952 people shopping in the town centre of Bradford on Avon were spoilt for choice with six greengrocers, four butchers, eight clothes or shoe shops, six sweet shops, four bakers, four hairdressers, four grocers and three chemists (within 100 yards of each other in Silver Street).

"We did go to Bath sometimes on the train – once a month. But then you went to buy something like a special dress. You didn't go and buy ordinary, everyday things." (WS12)

Rationing had begun in January 1940 but didn't end until well after the war was over. Indeed, some foods such as meat were more scarce in the late Forties and early Fifties than they had been during the war when Marshall Aid from the USA had been helping us out. Clothes rationing ended in 1949, sweets in 1953 and food restrictions were finally lifted in July 1954.

In 1952 the weekly rations were 2 ounces cheese (56 grams); 2 ounces tea (about 20 teabags today); 2 ounces jam spread; 4 ounces bacon or ham; 8 ounces sugar; 1 shilling's worth of meat; 8 ounces fats of which only 2 ounces could be butter. You had to choose a specific shop for each type of goods whether it be butcher, grocery or dairy, and then you were restricted to those shops as the shopkeepers got their supplies according to the number of their registered customers. Queuing was commonplace.

Meat substitutes such as Corned Beef and Spam (Supply Pressed American Meat or Spiced Ham, depending on which version you wish to believe) eked out the meagre allowance. Even basic foods like potatoes were highly sought after and, hard to believe now, were kept under the counter for regular customers![24]

"I suppose it was a time of austerity but at the time that was life, you just put up with it because you didn't know any better. Rationing was still very much on then and there was a lot more emphasis on growing stuff. Everybody had a garden and so grew their own vegetables. I only remember having meat and vegetables and that was it. There was nothing pre-packed or anything like that." (WS12)

Without refrigeration, housewives (invariably) shopped daily. Everything was cut, weighed and packed in brown paper bags – or blue for sugar. Biscuits were displayed in tilted tins – and the end one was always broken biscuits, much cheaper. The concept of self-service was being tried out at Woolworths' flagship store in London's Strand in 1952, but was unpopular with store managers expressing doubts about it being seen as 'un-British'.[25] It was all a long way from Bradford on Avon with its jangling shop door bells and shopkeepers totting up totals in their head.

"They were somebody, weren't they? They all had different personalities but you respected them, didn't you? You were a bit nervous of them. If you went in the shoe shop and Mr Uncles was actually in there . . . he wouldn't have served you but he'd have got his assistants to serve you. He was quite a firm sort of person, a proper business person." (CB12)

A resident remembers her experience of shopping as a child:

"That was the trouble in those days, children were sort of pushed to the back. That was another thing about going shopping, you'd be afraid that the grown-ups would push in front. You'd think, well, I was here first! Of course, we'd never say anything." (AB12)

Nowadays we have online ordering, supermarket deliveries and the local convenience store but what could be more convenient than having the baker bring a selection of bread straight to the door for you to pick the best of what was on offer? The grocer sent someone up to take your order personally and delivered the same day. The early morning chink of milk bottles was commonplace and home deliveries were made by the fishmonger, the coalman and the greengrocer.

However, the convenience of late night shopping was unheard of and Wednesday half-day closing was the norm. Wednesday afternoons felt as sleepy as Sundays. These were times when you could cross the road without looking and the current bottlenecks would have been regarded with astonishment. With an impressive three commercial garages in Bradford on Avon in 1952, there was still very little traffic. Despite the hills, many Bradfordians had bicycles and in those days children of eight and nine years set off to cycle to Westbury Hill for picnics without fear of accident. One resident recalled ruefully how different things were:

"I bought the property in Market Street with a loan from my father in 1963 for £1,100 and I remember asking him, before I bought it, to come over and meet me. I came down from London and he drove over from Cardiff and we stood in Market Street and we looked at the property from the other side of the road, standing in the road for about quarter of an hour on a Sunday afternoon, and I remember him saying 'Well, I hope there is some traffic and passing trade coming down this hill'. No traffic at all came down in the quarter hour we stood there. That was what Bradford on Avon was like on a Sunday in 1963." (AJ11)[26]

With so much local competition, Bradford's shopkeepers did their best to attract customers. One butcher recalled leaving the lights on in the shop overnight, with a couple of lamb carcasses hanging on display in the window. His boss called him up and instructed him to go back, switch the lights off and stop wasting electricity. He also tried sticking cut-out recipes from *People's Friend* in the window to inspire local housewives. The boss was not impressed and ordered them removed.

Marketing has come a long way since then and online shopping would have been beyond comprehension. In the 1950s, viral (or Vyrol) was something you took as a tonic, Spam was something you ate, hardware was nails and screws, and software – well, you would probably have been directed to the woollens department.

Prices have also changed beyond recognition. Not only is the terminology different, with decimal having elbowed out pounds, shillings and pence in 1971, but factoring in the lower salaries and cost of living in 1952, a straightforward calculation to current prices is more complicated. With an average weekly wage for men of around £9 and £5 for women, the housekeeping had to stretch a long way. Larger items such as furniture were priced in guineas, a posh way of indicating quality. Buying on the never-never was regarded as a no-no by many people who preferred the extraordinary concept of saving up until you could afford something such as a 14-inch television at £63, the equivalent today of £1,500 to £6,000 depending on how the relative worth is calculated. An explanation of current equivalent values is given on page 110.

Having tried to put Bradford's shops into some sort of context, it's high time we started walking! The Street Trail History begins near the Tourist Information Centre in Westbury Gardens.

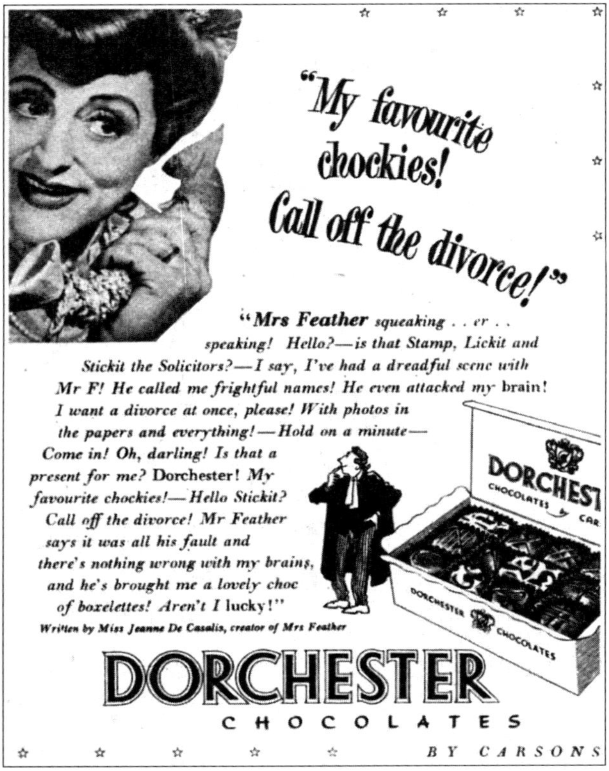

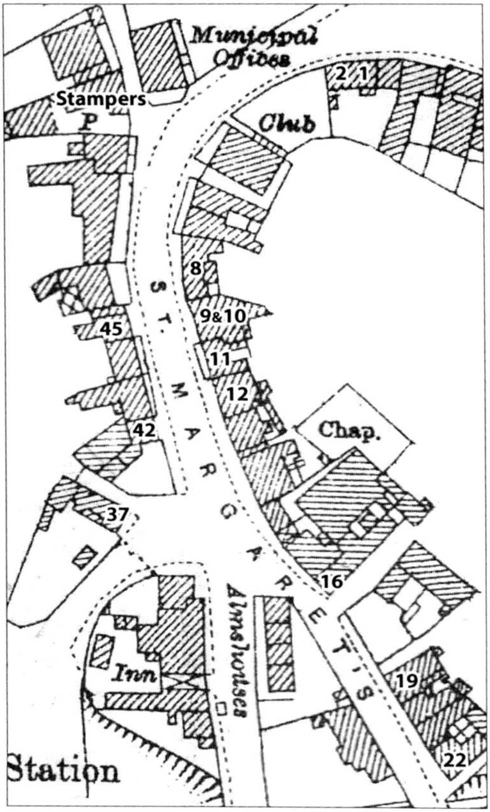

St Margaret's Street

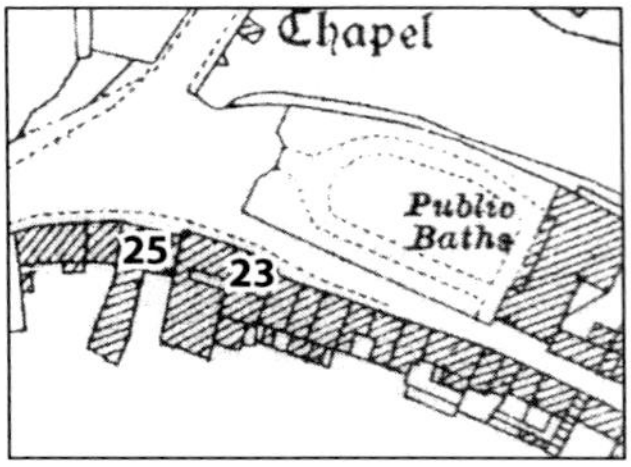

Bridge Street

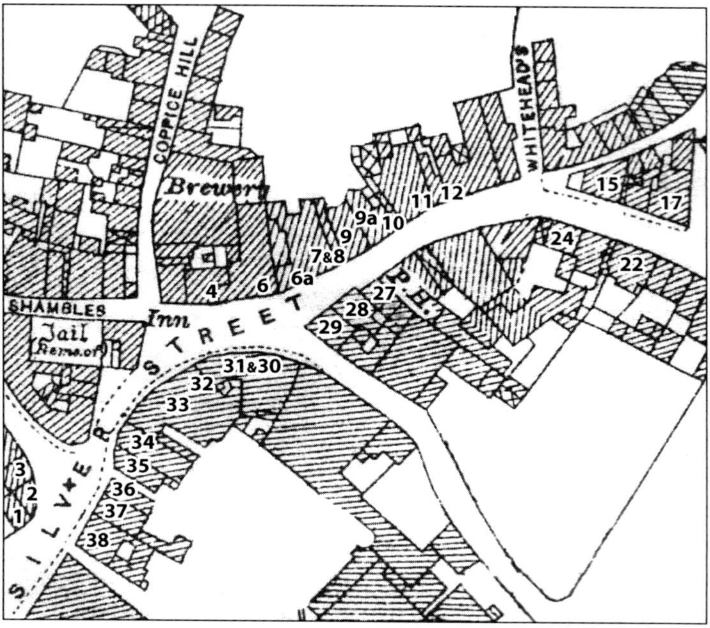

Silver Street

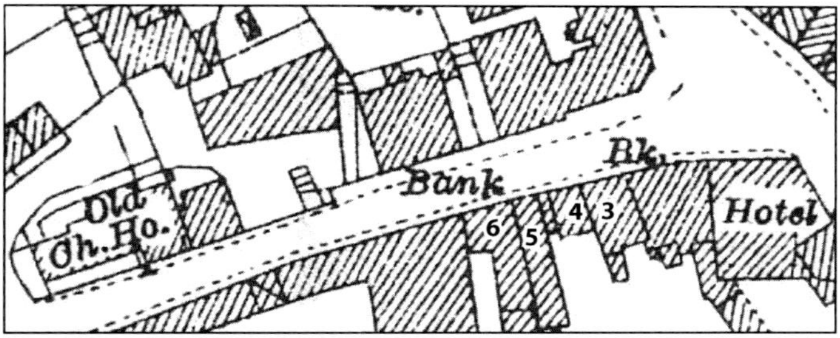

Church Street

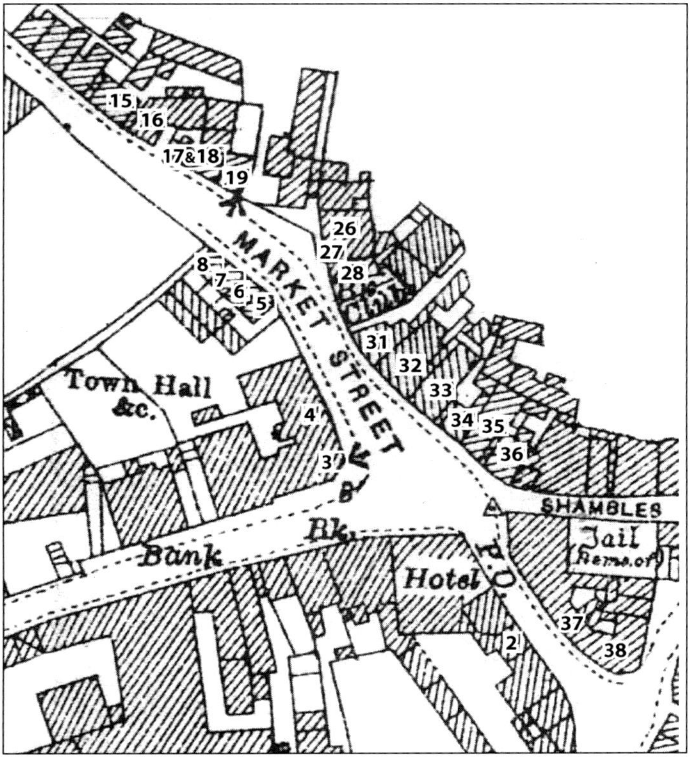

Market Street

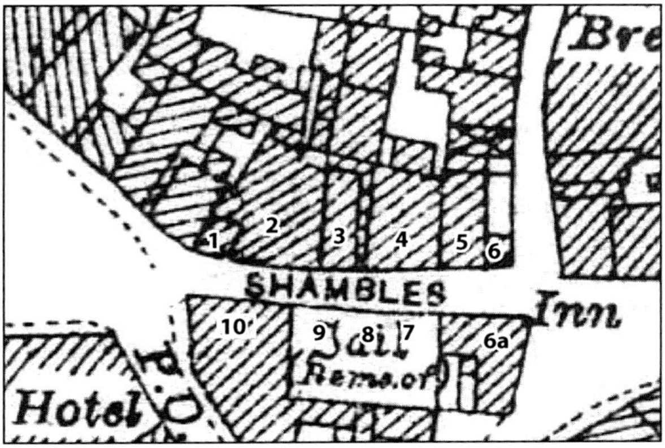

The Shambles

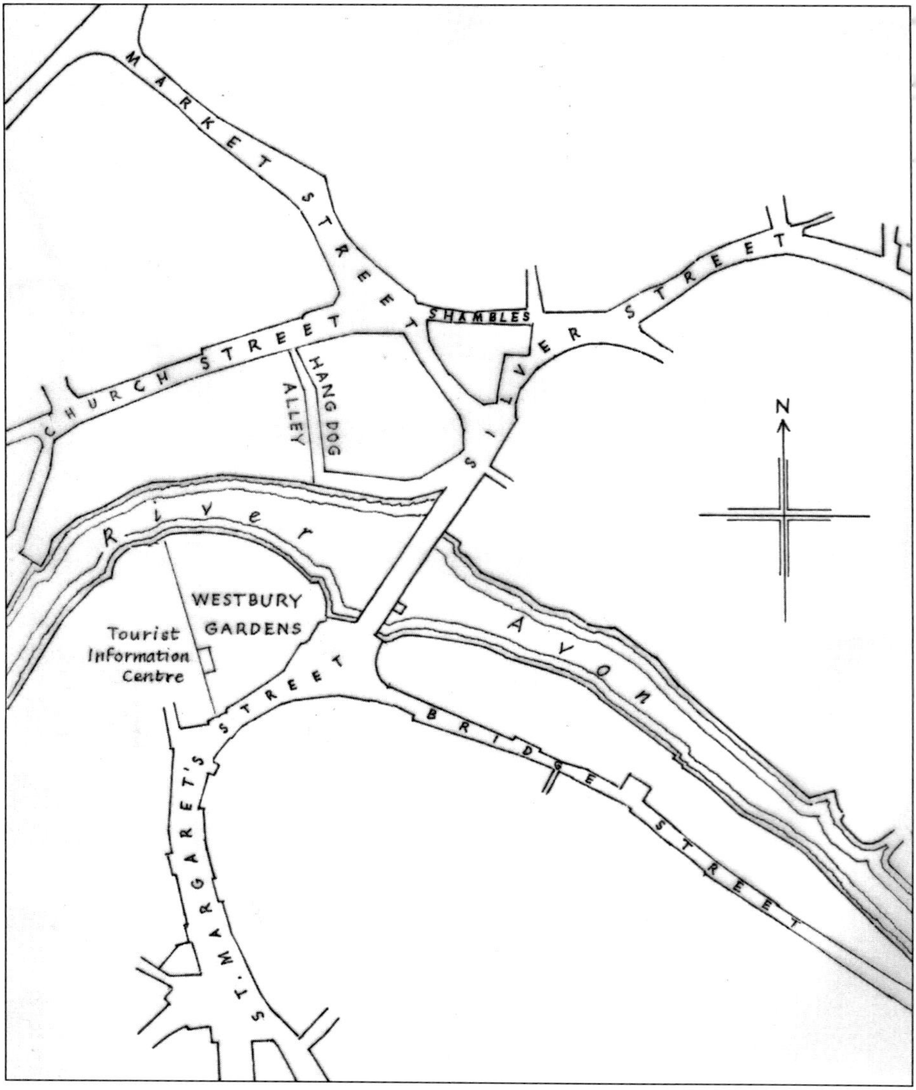
MARKET STREET
SHAMBLES
SILVER STREET
CHURCH STREET
HANG DOG ALLEY
N
River AVON
WESTBURY GARDENS
Tourist Information Centre
ST. MARGARET'S STREET
BRIDGE STREET

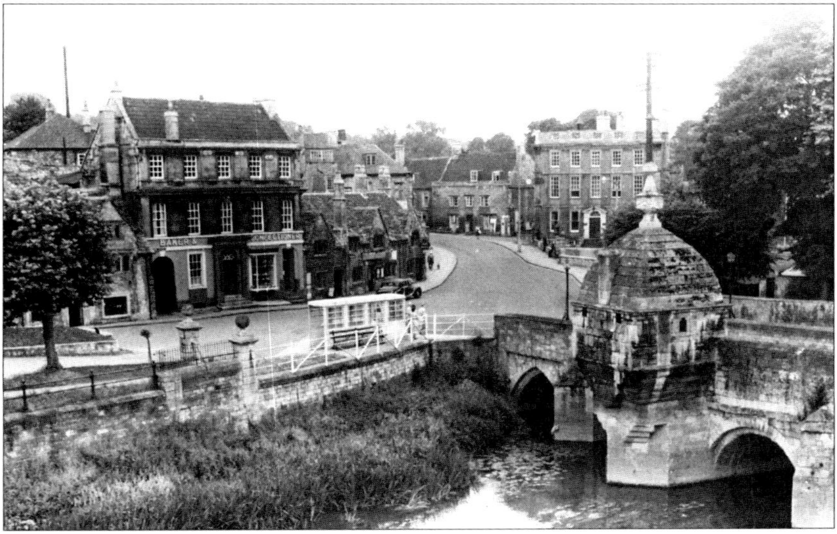

St Margaret's Street

~ This Bradford on Avon Street Trail begins at the Tourist Information Centre. The first section follows the road which leads away from the river alongside Westbury Gardens then curves up the hill into St Margaret's Street ~

The road is named after St Margaret's leper hospital which was founded nearby in 1235. It was the main street into town from the south, leading to the broad ford across the river.

In 1791 this was the scene of conflict between a mob of five hundred irate mill workers and Mr Phelps, a prominent clothier in the town who lived in Westbury House, the large house alongside Westbury Gardens. The mob demanded he hand over a scribbling horse he had squirrelled away in his basement, a new piece of carding technology which threatened their jobs. The house was pelted with stones; he returned with gunfire and a man, woman and child were killed. Unsurprisingly, far from subduing the mood, this action inflamed the crowd. The scribbler was eventually given up and triumphantly burnt on the bridge.[27]

Cattle and horse fairs were held here from at least the early nineteenth century.

A letter dating from 1885 gives a fascinating insight into the life of the town. Daniel Batchelor emigrated to America but wrote back to the local paper with memories of his life here in the 1830s, including this insight into horse dealing.

> *The cattle and horse fairs then extended from Timbrells* [the woollen dyers in the St Margaret's Hall building], *on St Margaret`s Street, up to the old poorhouse beyond the Cross Keys* [where the railway bridge is now on the Frome Road]. *I once heard the superintendent of the poor house - old-Bummy Ferris - expostulate with a jockey who was enraged at the nefarious work of stimulating an old mare with ginger quid's. It was a colloquy between the two men not soon to be forgotten, and even now, as I write 'n, provokes a spasm of laughter not easily suppressed.*[28]

And the 'ginger quid's' referred to? According to the 1811 *Dictionary of the Vulgar Tongue*, 'to feague a horse is to put ginger up a hose's fundament, and formerly, as it is said, a live eel, to make him lively and carry his tail well.' Hardly surprising the old mare was frisky. It must all have been hugely entertaining for the many straw bonnet makers who had colonised this part of town according to the census of 1841.[29] The horse might well have been waiting to get through the turnpike which was situated near here by the Old Baptist Chapel. The tariff due in 1841 was one penny and 'For every drove of oxen, cows or neat cattle, tenpence per score'.[30]

One hundred years later, in the 1950s, the trade in horses had been replaced by car dealers, with three garages here in St Margaret's Street.

Stampers Garage

In 1952 Stampers Garage was located in what is now the entrance to St Margaret's car park in old buildings alongside the corner house at number 48. Now demolished, they had previously been part of the weaving and dyeing business in the St Margaret's Hall building.

This was the first garage in Bradford on Avon. Mr Gerald Stamper introduced the first charabanc and ran a village bus service.

> *"The Fire Brigade headquarters was in the car park then. We used to get petrol at Stampers. If you wanted a Morris car you got it at Stampers Garage. If you wanted an Austin, you had to go round the corner to Stones. You could walk across the road without looking because you could hear them coming. There were lots of people on bikes of course but lots of people always walking in those days."* (CB12)

In 1952, one of the bestselling cars, the Austin A40 Devon, cost around £685, depending onhow you calculate it, equivalent to between £16,000 and £51,000 in today's money – (see page 110 for an explanation of conversion), a staggering amount compared to wages at the time. But petrol was the equivalent of just 11p a litre – and you would have had the thrill of reaching 60 mph in an impressive 37 seconds.[31]

> *"In those days there was no traffic about, hardly. Dad had a car when we were quite small but you'd come down and you'd hardly see any cars. People would only go out I suppose weekends because people worked in Bradford and could find a job in Bradford, so of course they walked to work, they didn't drive to work and they probably couldn't afford the petrol anyway."* (AB12)

Despite the encouraging motto, "Service...and satisfaction", the garage was demolished in the early 1960s when the car park was built.

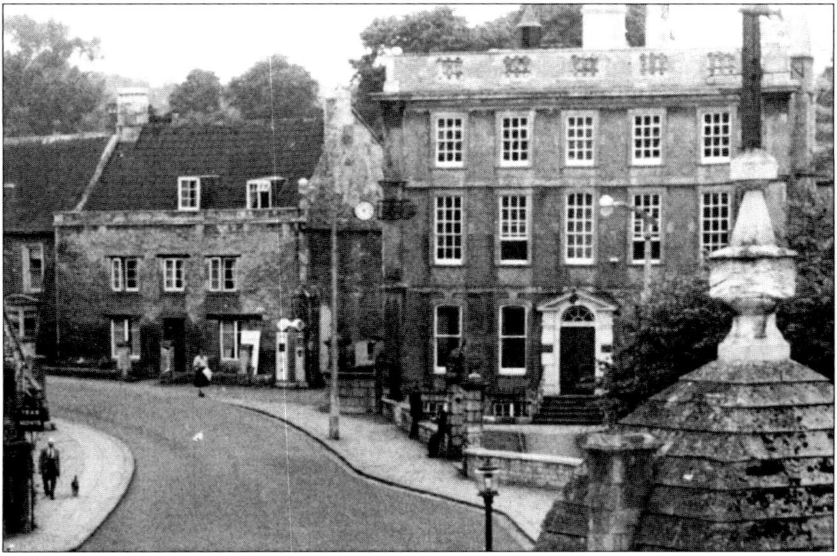

No. 45 Young's Stationers

In 1952 this was a stationers run by F G Young. The shop was a newsagent back in 1907.

> *"It was a newsagent for many, many years,"* recalls JB, who ran the business here in the Sixties.

> *"We had about twenty boys delivering papers all over Bradford, going up the hills and everywhere. There was nowhere in Bradford we didn't go to. It was a nightmare*

to organise every day, especially in the bad weather. But anyway, if they didn't turn up I had to go out with it. So there you go. Most people, you know, nine out of ten people, took a newspaper." (JB12)

In those days popular magazines such as *Reveille* and *Titbits*, 3 pence in 1952 (about 1p now), were full of ideas for the busy housewife on how to run her household with knitting, sewing and cooking tips. Retractable ball pens had only just come out in 1949 and were a huge novelty, selling for 9 pence (4p).

The shops now between numbers 45 and the corner grocers were all private houses in the 1950s.

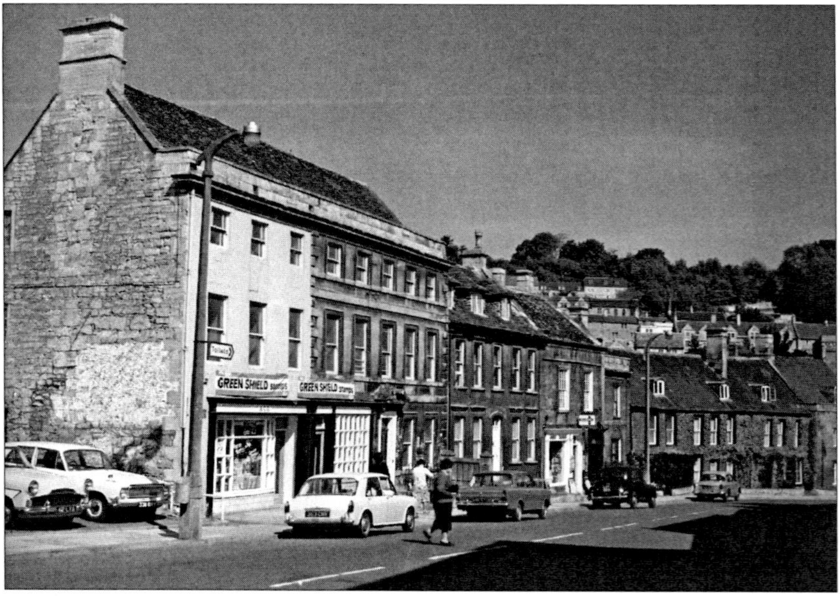

St Margaret's Street, 1960s

No. 42 Keates Garage

In 1952 the corner shop was Keates Garage, a successful business which had been established in 1910 by Donald Keates, trading as Perkins & Keates Motorcycles. His brothers Reginald and Ronald took it over when he was killed in the First World War. They built up a Model T Ford taxi service in conjunction with their charabanc business and in 1922 boasted the first hearse in Bradford, a stately Armstrong Siddeley Sapphire. They moved to new premises in the Frome Road in 1962.

The entrance to the garage went straight through what is now the ground floor of the Grocery Basket. Cars pulled up outside for petrol served from pumps on the pavement. The rubber hose swung round over the heads of pedestrians walking by.

Alongside the garage was a row of dilapidated 17th century houses which were demolished in 1935 leaving a space which awaits development.

~ The Street Trail crosses Station Road to the fish and chip shop ~

No. 37 Stones' Station Garage

In 1952 Stones Garage had premises on both sides of the corner of Station Road, with the showroom where the fish and chip restaurant is now. Founded by Edward William Stone in 1919, the garage continued after his death in 1940, and by 1952 it was owned by the same people who owned Stampers Garage just down the road. The garage finally closed in 2006. Car ownership doubled in the 1950s and by 1955 over three million cars had been sold. Prices were steep and by 1959 only 32% of households owned a car.

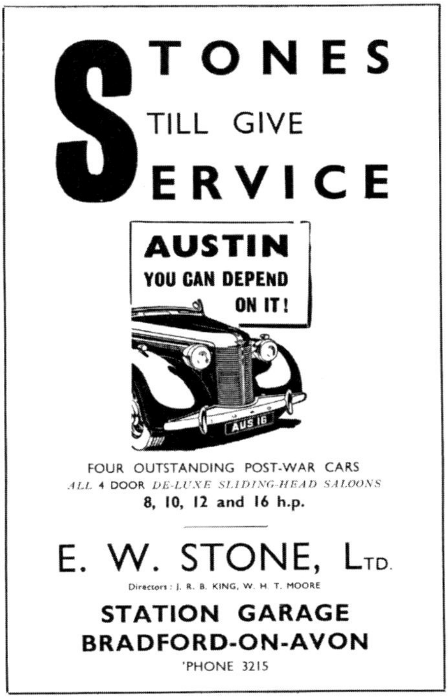

"There weren't many cars in those days. When we moved down here my father was told very sternly by his boss that if he chose to live in Bradford on Avon which was three miles away from Trowbridge it was his entire responsibility to get in and out and there was no way that they would cover any of the cost of it!" (RS12)

~ The Street Trail crosses Frome Road and St Margaret's Street by the old Almshouses, crosses St Margaret's Hill, before continuing 50 metres along St Margaret's Street to number 22 ~

In the Fifties the local residents here were spoilt for choice with three small grocers within yards of each other. Each had its own loyal clientele and so got by.

No. 22 Pearce's Grocers

In 1952 the house at number 22 was Mrs Pearce's. *"Shoppers were loyal in those days; you had your regulars you'd get to know over the years,"* recalls a former shopkeeper. Numbers 21 and 20 have both existed as shops but were not trading in the 1950s.

~ The Trail returns back down St Margaret's Street towards the centre of town ~

No. 19 Mrs Hurst's Stores

Although listed as Don's Stores, the shop was run by a nice lady who had a soft spot for the children desperately hunting down the few sweets available in town – sweet rationing did not end until 1953.

> *"On a Saturday afternoon we used to go round to the sweet shops with our coupons to see who had sweets. Well, quite often they didn't have any - 'I'm sorry, nothing!' Well, we'd walk up towards Trowbridge Road, there were two shops there. One was a little sweet shop, and of course we used to do it on a regular sort of basis to try and get some sweets of a Saturday because we then used to walk to Trowbridge to the films, and of course she got to know us and she used to come out and say 'No, I haven't any sweets' in a loud voice just in case there was anybody else coming in - and then she'd whisper, 'Would you like some chocolate drops?' and she'd say 'Hang on' and she used to come out with something, some jellies or whatever. She used to put some back as a rule because she got to know us. 'There's the girls coming in again'"* (JS12)

This was one of six sweet shops in Bradford's town centre in the early Fifties.

No. 16 Rose's Grocers

On the corner of St Margaret's Street and St Margaret's Hill was Rose's Grocery.

> *"It was just a little grocery shop. Just general everyday things that you wanted, you know. It probably was the last in Bradford that actually closed down before people changed to other ideas".* (JB11)

In 1909 it had been occupied by Henry Burgess, a popular baker in the town, who took it over from his mother. He might well have been a son of the Mr Burgess who ran a bakers a few doors down at number 12 in the 1890s, and seen in the photograph on page 34 with his brothers and sisters, the window now much altered.

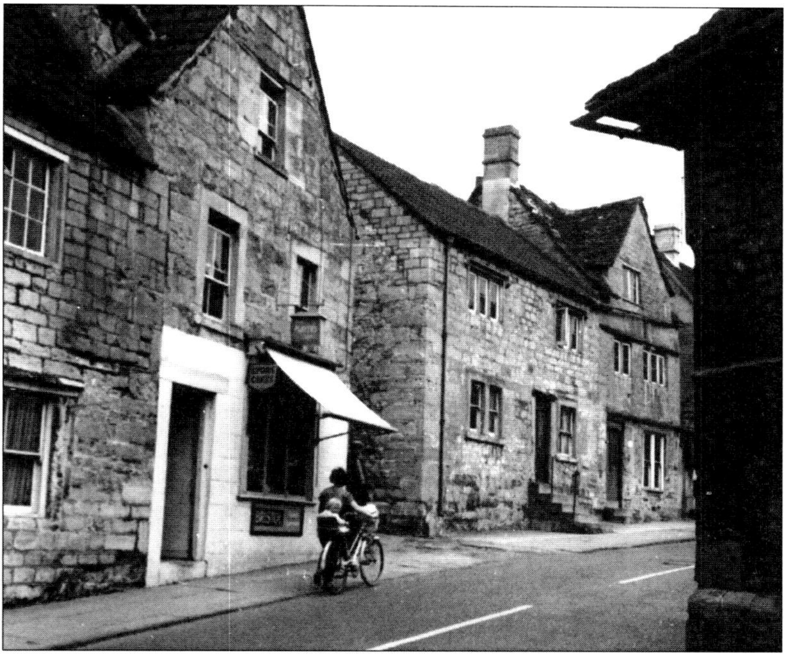

No. 12 The Co-operative Shoe Shop

In 1952 the double-fronted betting shop was one of eight Co-op shops in the town at that time:

> *"He used to make a beautiful parcel with the shoe box and brown paper and a string handle. You were so proud of your shoes all done up in brown paper. The Co-op offices were on the floor above, used to be a gents tailors."* (JS12)

The Co-op was founded in Bradford in 1861 and by the 1930s had eight shops in the town, supplying almost every need imaginable. The Co-operative movement was a force to be reckoned with. By 1958 there were 30,000 Co-ops nationally, with 12 million members, the highest number in its history. At one point Bradford on Avon was believed to be second only to Rochdale, Lancashire – home of the Co-op movement – for the number of Co-op shops trading in a single town.[33] Its popularity declined through the 1960s as other retail outlets began to rival it and in 1988, after 121 years of business in Bradford, the Co-op's last two shops at 33 Silver Street (the grocers) and 37 Silver Street (the butchers) finally closed. The building dates to the 18th century and was occupied for about fifty years from 1848 onwards by James Duck, Master Baker, his wife and four children. Another family of butchers, the Burgesses, were there in the 1890s. It was the Midland Railway Office until 1908, conveniently close to the station and goods yard. In the 1960s the Co-op shoe shop closed down and the local firm of Moulton Bicycles took over the premises as a showcase for their pioneering bicycle design which was launched in 1952 and went on to break world records. The models in the photographer are two high-end designs, the Speedsix and the Deluxe.

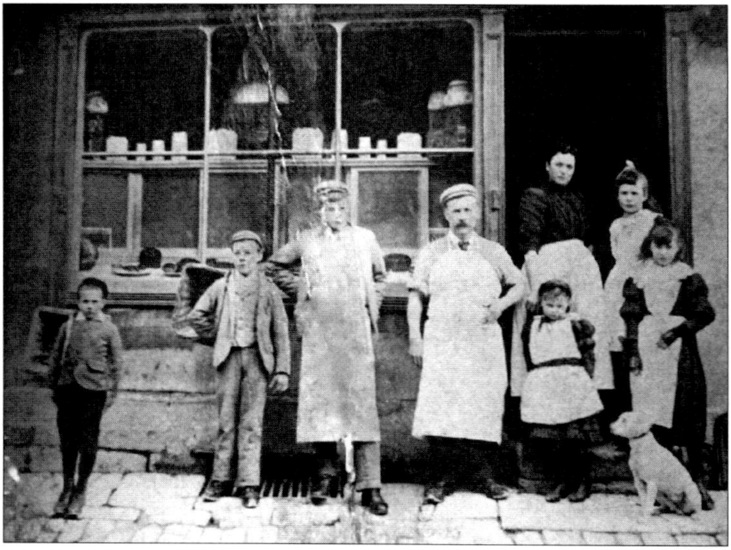

The Burgess family bakers, 1890s

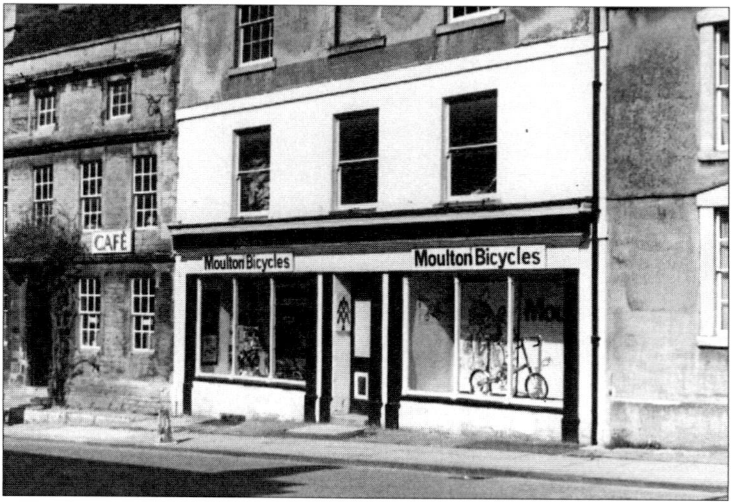

Moulton Bicycles window in the 1960s

No. 11 The Green Tree Café

In 1952 Mrs Anderson and her daughter Mary were running a busy café here:

> *"They had a cafe on two floors, on the right hand side as you went in, kitchens on the left. She used to do outside catering for functions. She was the one in Bradford everyone went to."* (CB12)

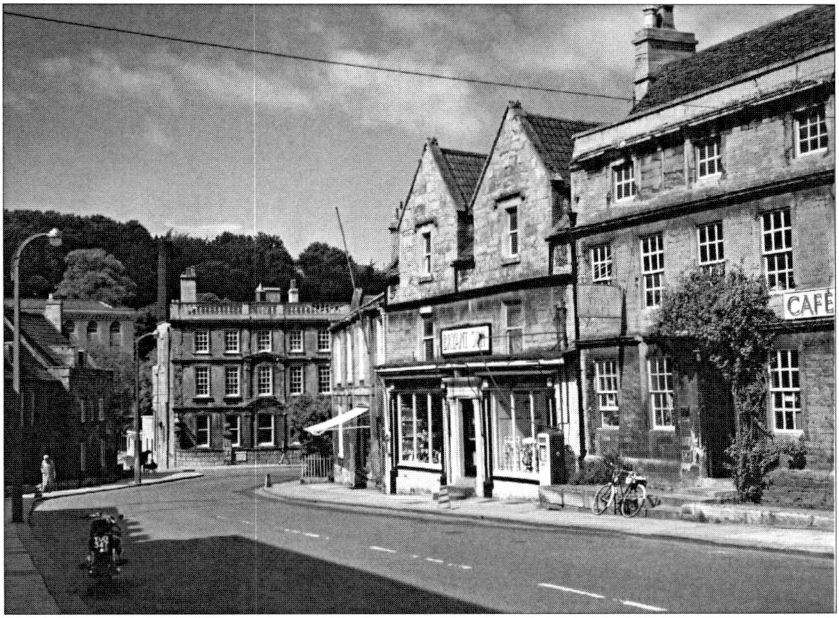

> *"That was lovely, a dear little cafe. And some nice people that ran it. Sort of homely feeling in there."* (JS12)

> *"She did my wedding reception. When I was working at the Co-op we'd go up there for a lovely lunch for seven shillings and sixpence (38p)and you might even have had three courses, that was in the Sixties. Money went a long way."* (AB12)

Nos. 9 & 10 Bryants Hardware Store

In 1952 Mr Bryant supplied hardware from this twin gabled house, now a restaurant. He started the shop in 1923 and built up a very successful business, covering the outlying villages with a travelling shop in a horse and cart in the 1920s and '30s, and then in an adapted Model T Ford.

> *"They had a mobile van like a little shop and you bought things like Brasso and*

dusters and brooms." (WS12)

His range of stock was astonishing. Everything the hard-pressed housewife needed and delivered to the door. Larger items were discussed beforehand and a range of products brought out the following week for inspection.

> *"They used to take a lot of orders. They might order a rug: they'd say I want a rug for the bedroom, will you bring me some to see. They'd ask about size and colour and we'd put perhaps half a dozen on the van for them to have a look at."* (NC92)[34]

> *"His raison d'etre was the delivery of paraffin. Basically it was a converted ambulance, ex-army thing with a tank on the back and they dispensed paraffin and drove round the town with it on the back."* (RS12)

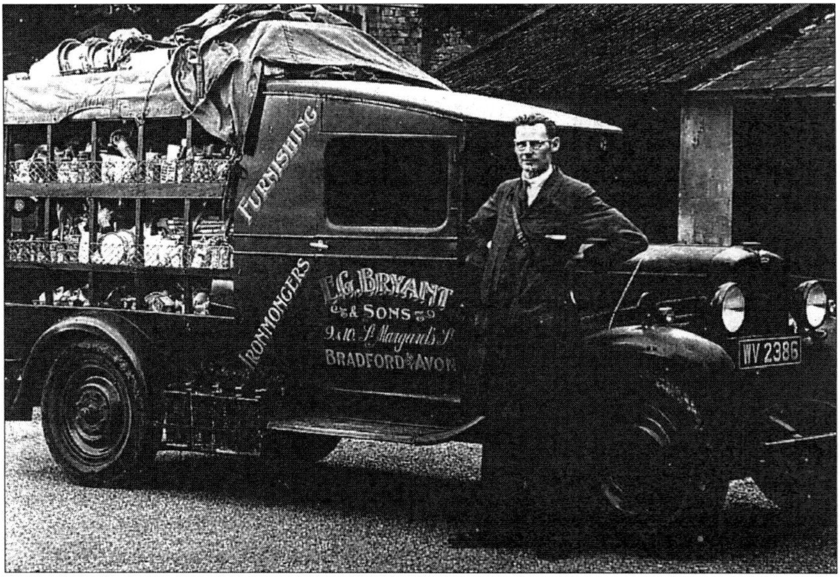

Mr Les Bryant and his travelling shop

Originally one house built early in the 17th century, the building was divided around 1700, and then reconnected some time in the 20th century. The left side was occupied by the Plume of Feathers in the 18th century and then the French Horn inn early in the 19th century when it was allegedly built as a hostelry for French prisoners of war working on the final stretch of the Kennet and Avon Canal. Since then it has housed a coal dealer, a shoemaker, and a grocer and tallow chandler with his boiling house and candle store in the yard behind. The Long family of builders, whose descendants still trade as builders today, occupied the other side of the house. The building also housed a succession of photographers, possibly starting with Frederick Shettle, trading as The Fine Art Photo Co. H & G Morse were there in 1911 with a photographic studio up in the attic.[35]

Bryants closed in around 2001 and the shop sign is now on display in the Bradford on Avon Museum.

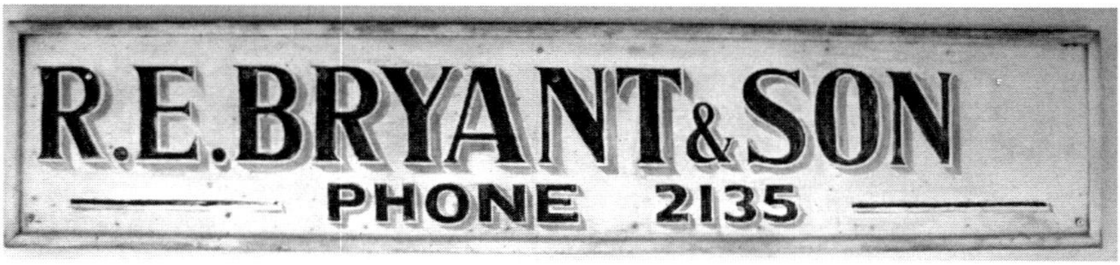

No. 8 Rossiter's Electrical Shop

In 1952 this shop was owned by William Herbert Rossiter who had set up the business over twenty years previously. He was the Chief Fire Officer during the war but found time to operate a jazz radio station from the shop basement on Sundays, a routine which could well have continued into the 1950s. Entertainment was in his blood. His father, Herbert Rossiter, founded the Bradford on Avon Cinema Company in 1930. William Rossiter sold the business to Mr Binding in 1964 and, very sadly, died just three months later at the start of his retirement.

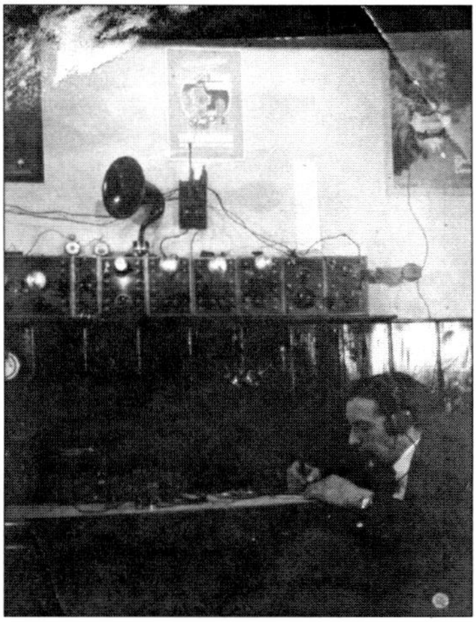

William Rossiter broadcasting his live jazz station from the basement of his shop

> *"He was quite a pillar of society, Mr Rossiter. The shopkeepers of those days, they were all thought of quite highly, which you certainly don't get nowadays."* (WS12)

Built in 1826 on land owned by Zachariah Shrapnel, the house replaced three earlier gabled cottages. Zachariah was related to Lieutenant-General Henry Shrapnel who invented shrapnel in 1784. In 1841 it was a grocers shop and in 1920 was occupied by a tailor.[36]

→ Look for . . . the beautiful 1930s glass shop sign advertising Radio & Television and Electrical Installations. This shop has another authentic detail – the yellow plastic film to prevent goods in the window from fading ←

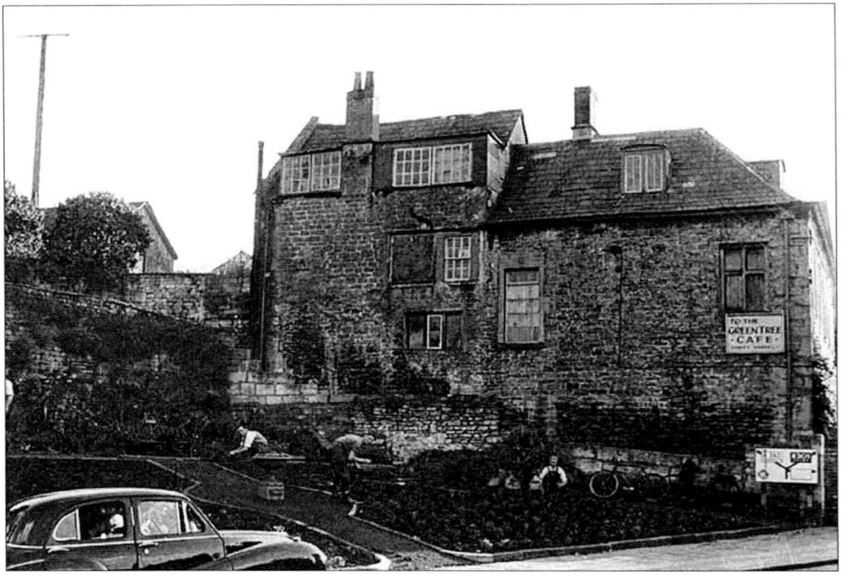

Nos. 1 & 2 The Three Gables Café

In 1952 this was a popular café with a sweet shop tucked in on the left side of the row of three 17th century houses. Butcher Bert Scrine and the Co-op confectioner Edie Baxter moved here after they married in the 1930s and converted the building into The Three Gables café. Bert Scrine was related to the Scrines chemists of Silver Street. The garden alongside, seen in the photograph, was maintained by the husband of Madame Soul, who ran the ladies outfitters and drapers in Market Street.

> *"They knew our family quite well and if we wanted to get a wafer of ice cream, we'd get a bigger one. They used to cut it up out of the block and it seemed extra big! I always remember when my parents went away for the day, they'd send me over there to get my lunch. They'd look after us and it was just a traditional, you know, one o'clock family meal in their little cafe there."* (CB12)

In the days when 'fridges were considered a luxury commodity rather than a necessity, ice cream was wrapped in layers of newspaper and carried home at high speed.

"We used to go to the Congregational Chapel and afterwards we were allowed to go and buy a wafer, but we had to bring it home to eat it so we didn't get it on our Sunday Best clothes!" (AB12)

In 1861 the Queen's Head was situated in the right hand part of this building. The left hand side was occupied in 1911 by Mrs Barnett, tea and coffee house keeper.

~ The Street Trail follows this row of buildings into Bridge Street ~

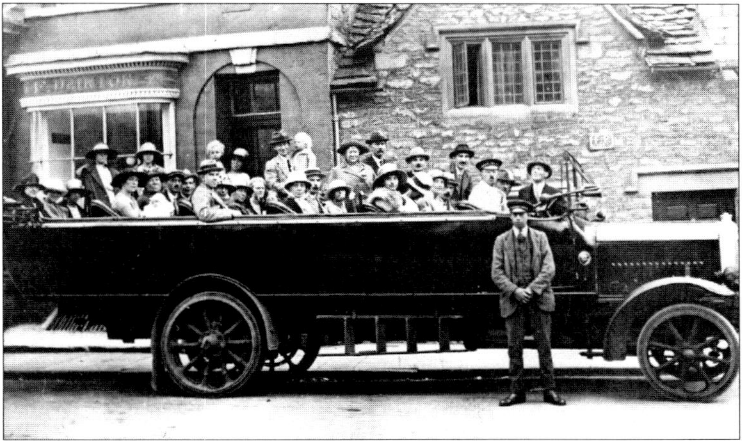

Stampers charabanc in Bridge Street in the 1920s

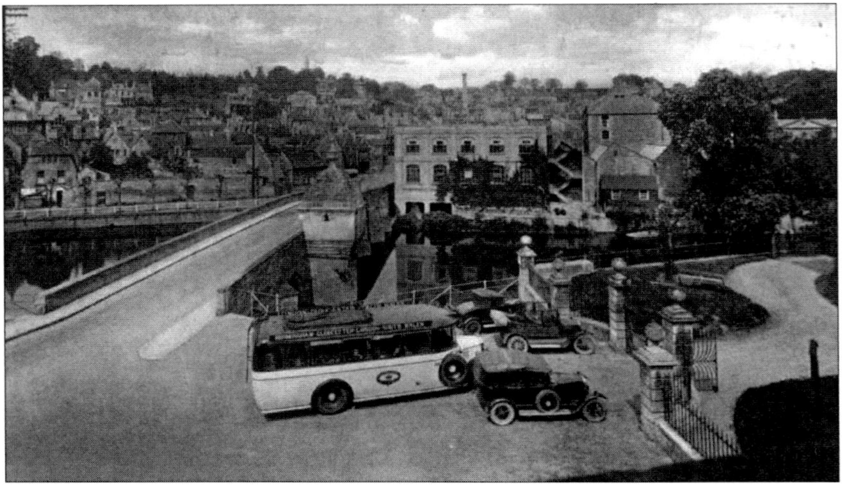

Bridge Street

This part of town looked quite different in the 1950s. The car park and library site was occupied by the Memorial Baths and gardens, built by John Moulton to commemorate Queen Victoria's Diamond Jubilee in 1897 at a time when many people were without baths in their own homes.

Local residents remember them well. Prices for the public swimming baths varied according to how clean the water was. It was changed twice a week, by which time you could hardly see the floor tiles. The spring water was carried by pipe all the way from Ladywell in Newtown. It crossed the river by Westbury Gardens and you can still see water bubbling up from leaks in the pipe at this point.[37] The baths were demolished in 1965.

No. 25 Phillips Baker & Confectioner

This imposing three-storey Georgian house was Mr Phillips Bakers in 1952, continuing a long history of bakers on this site dating back to 1732. In the 1950s the grand front entrance led into the family home and the entrance to the bakery was around the back.

> *"I remember going down to collect bread, through the archway – there was an opening where you asked for your bread and paid for it."* (RS12)

"They had a tiny little man and he had a huge basket and he ran everywhere. There must have been a van of some sort, I suppose, but he would come rushing in with his huge basket, a very cheery fellow, whistling and so on." (WS12)

" We used to go to the swimming baths about seven o'clock in the morning and we used to call in to the bakers and get some hot bread rolls and bring them home and put loads of butter or margarine on them as that's all we had in those days." (CB12)

Mr Phillips bought the business from Frank Dainton who had taken over from his father in 1916 when Bradford had an astonishing choice of 11 bakeries. It was here that Mr Dainton baked the bread that was handed out to the poor of the parish around 1900. Going back even earlier, the building was occupied by William Miles, baker and maltster in 1732.

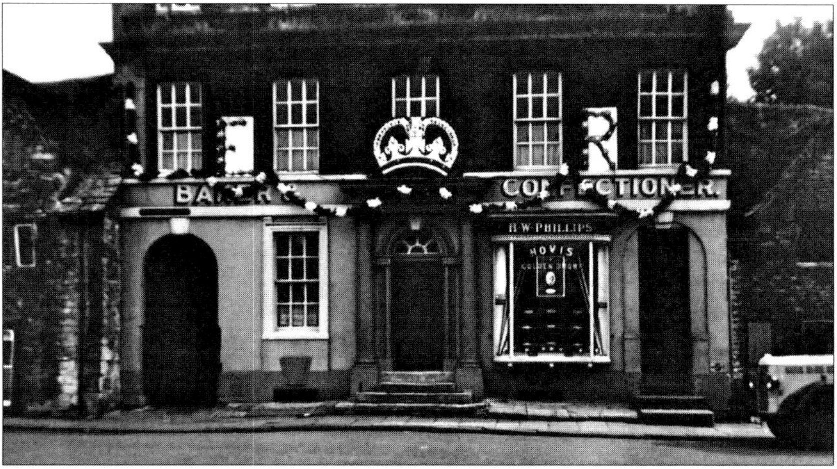

Phillips Bakers celebrating the Coronation in 1953

No. 23 Lailey's Forge

The old twin-gabled house next door, now a café, was home to the Lailey family in 1952 when Ken Lailey was running his blacksmith and wheelwright's business in the stone building beyond on the right. His father Albert Lailey opened a forge here in 1918 and they lived in the old house shown in the photograph on page 42. This was the last remaining forge in West Wiltshire, finally closing in the 1980s.

"Gwen Lailey remembers the forge when there'd be up to four horses at a time waiting to be shod and Bridge Street crowded with gypsy caravans, passing through on their way up to the Bradford Leigh fair held on the last Monday in

August. More general iron work and wheelwrighting was done on the first floor above the forge."[38]

The local children found it a great attraction, fascinated by the fire and acrid fumes as the hot shoe was applied to the horse's hoof.

Records show there was a forge in Bridge Street as long ago as 1820.

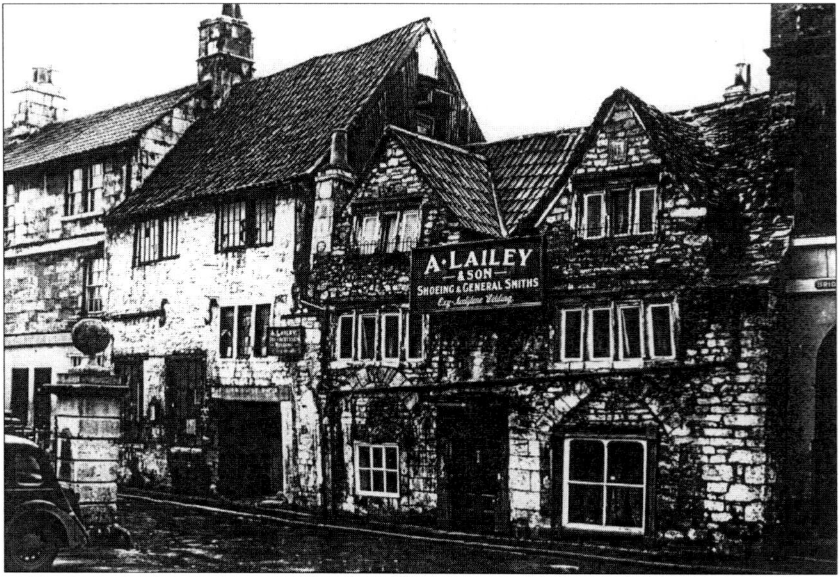

This had been a run-down area of the town, cluttered with old carpenters' and wheelwrights' workshops and two iron foundries. From the path by the river you can see the two 13th century ribbed and pointed arches on the east side of the bridge, still today the only river crossing in the centre of town, apart from the pedestrian bridge beside St Margaret's Hall constructed in 1962. The ford which crossed the river on the west side and dating back to at least 652AD was still in use in the 1800s.

→ **Look for ... the letters JM on the railings alongside the river, commemorating John Moulton who commissioned the Baths. The Moulton family had established a successful rubber industry in the town in 1848 and a descendant, Dr Alex Moulton, went on to invent the Moulton bike in the 1950s** ←

~ The Street Trail now crosses the bridge ~

The small building on the bridge had various uses over the years, from chapel to lock up to armaments store. It was also used as a toll house, collecting dues on animals crossing the bridge on their way to market.[39]

→ Look for . . . the small rings on the side of the bridge, believed to have been where cattle were tethered on their way to market [40] ←

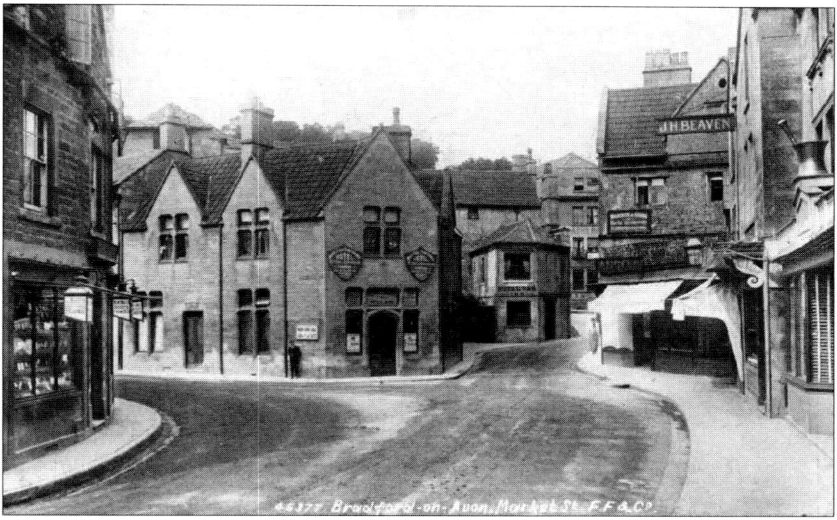

One solitary small boy is the only sign of life in this deserted scene at the junction of Market Street and Silver Street, c. 1900

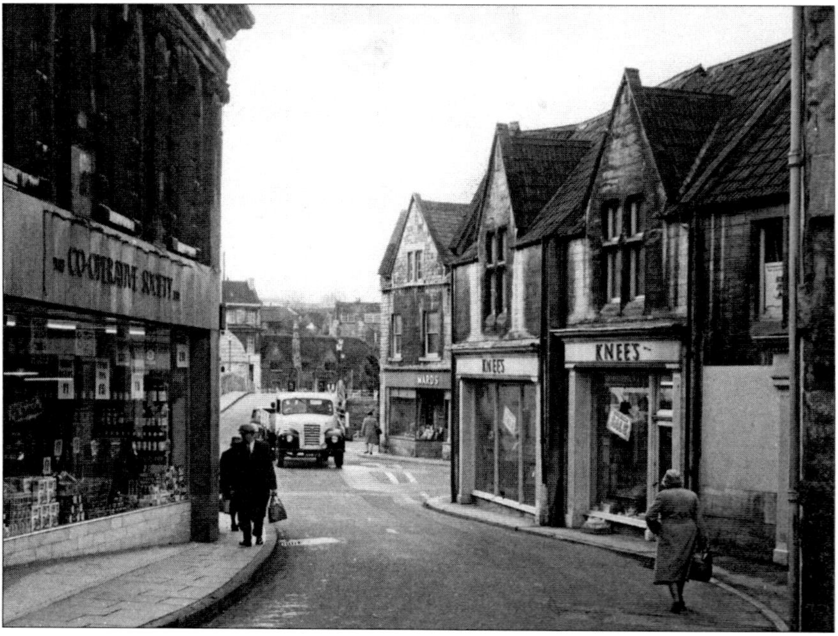

Silver Street

Crossing over the bridge from south to north into Silver Street, this first short stretch of road was known as Bridgefoot in the 19th century. Many towns have a Silver Street. It was the name given to the street which leads to the town market, as in this case.

The market place was situated where Silver Street meets the Shambles and until 1820 housed the old Market Hall with its butchers' stalls and whipping post.

The market moved to Pippet Street (now Market Street) in 1841 but Silver Street remained the main road into the town from the north and east up until the early part of the twentieth century.

Here on the east side of the bridge and very close to the river's edge was an old building which housed Mrs G Crisp listed in 1886 as a greengrocer, then in 1899 Edward Butcher, shopkeeper. Next door was the Lamb Inn, demolished in 1919 to make way for a new mill building, now part of the Kingston Mill development. The Lamb Inn was an imposing building with a portico supporting a carved stone lamb, long since destroyed by vandals in the grounds of The Hall, recalled Bertram Niblett.[41]

No. 38 Willson's Chemists

The first 1950s shop after the bridge on the right has also disappeared. Willson's Chemist filled the gap between the supermarket and the shops on the other side of the entrance to Kingston Mill. Well established in 1952, it was demolished in 1961 to widen the access to the Avon Rubber factory. Walter Henry Willson ran the business from 1887 until his death in 1931, when his son, Harry Courtenay Willson, took over.

A resident remembers it well from when he was a small boy:

> *"If you cut your foot when you were paddling in the river by the Town Bridge you used to hobble into Mr Willson and get it bandaged up. Mr Willson's was the place where you used to go and buy your bottle of sherry. Father always sent Mother to buy his bottle of sherry."* (CB12)

> *"There was a very narrow entrance down the side into the rubber factory and we used to watch lorries backing in. This was the main way into the Black Hole, as they used to call it. It's where they used to mix all the tyre stuff up, the rubber mix, everything was black. You used to get a film on the cars. People didn't worry so much in those days, did they? You used to see the chaps stood on the pavement, having a cigarette, absolutely black. No health and safety."* (CB12)

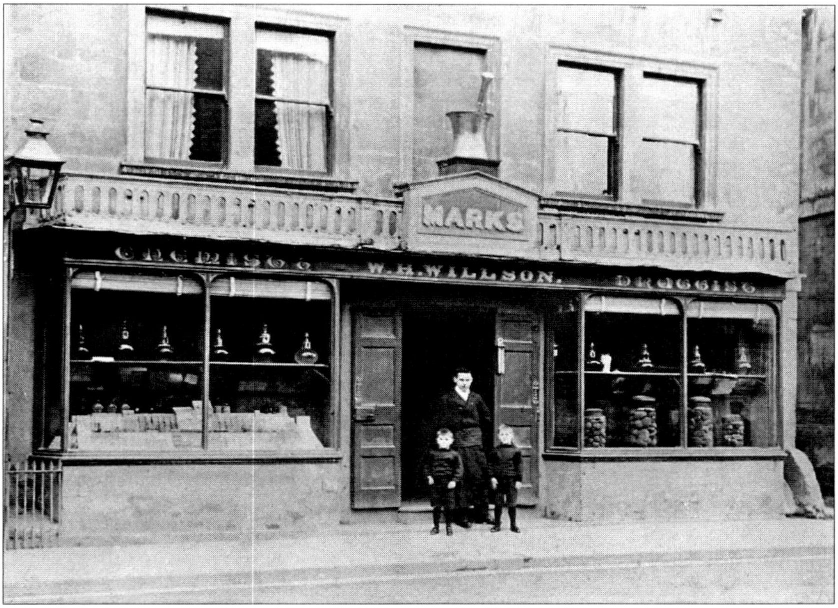

Walter Willson's assistant and his two sons, 1890s

There was a chemist here even earlier. Local boy George Marks set up the business in 1841 when he was only 20 and installed a giant pestle and mortar on a plinth above the door. It had gone by the 1950s and was known to have been in the tithe barn at Barton Farm for a time but has long since disappeared. In 1952 a jar of Pond's cleansing cream cost 3s.6d. (18p) and a bar of Pear's soap 10½d (4p).

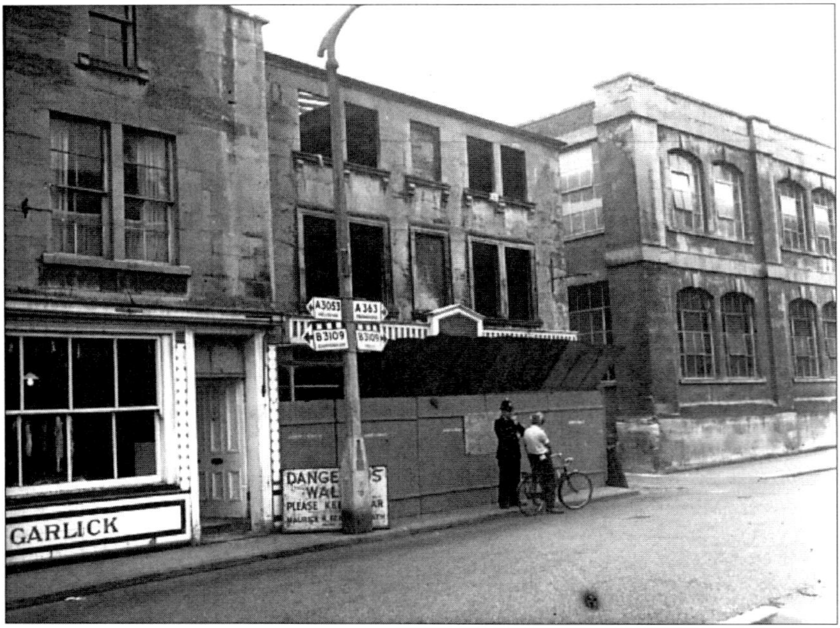

Willson's chemists during demolition in 1961, with the narrow entrance to Avon Rubber on the right and Garlick Butchers on the left

No. 37 The Co-operative Butchers

In 1952 the corner shop by the entrance to Kingston Mill was the last in a line of butchers on this site stretching back to 1867. With three other butchers in the centre of town, there was strong competition amongst the shopkeepers and they jealously guarded their customers who would have been paying 2s.8d., (14p) for a pound of rump steak.

> *"Mother used to say can you go down and get the meat for me and I used to come down about 8 o'clock on a Saturday morning and stand in the queue to get the meat. They were always obliging in there."* (JS12)

But not everyone found them so helpful…

"I can remember going for my grandmother because she liked to have a stew made from pork bones. I didn't like going in there because for some reason they didn't like selling them! I think it's because she wanted them with a bit of meat on them!" (AB12)

In the 1930s there was an abattoir round the back. Animals were driven up the passageway alongside the shop next door and a resident of the town who was a child at the time recalled the awful smell as the hair was singed off the pig carcasses. George Rose was the canny shopkeeper here in 1885. He appears to have combined the complementary trades of Butcher, Manure Agent and Seedsman. In 1911 it was Garlick & Sons, and the sign has been preserved behind the current façade.

No. 36 Browns Fruiterers and Wet Fish

In 1952 this was a busy greengrocers and wet fish shop, one of six greengrocers in the centre of Bradford at this time.

The fish lay on a marble slab inside the window, with shelves outside on the pavement displaying fruit and vegetables.

There were four separate and very heavy windows which had to be lifted out each day.

The fish would arrive twice a week from Grimsby and Hull, arriving early in the morning at the train station. It would be laid in ice in the shop window and as the ice slowly melted, the water drained away along a gully and down through the floor.

Before that there was a shoemaker on this site in 1848, then a milliner and drapers until 1899.

→ **Look for . . . the iron bar which kept the windows in place, now covered with many layers of paint, and the pipe which drained away the melting ice from the fish display** ←

No. 35 The Co-operative Furniture Department

In 1952 the furniture department of the Co-op occupied a building which was demolished in 1972, leaving an open space alongside the café. The shop had closed in the 1960s.

In 1867 this space was occupied by George Smith Ironmongers until 1885, and then Frederick Angell Boot and Shoemaker from 1886 to 1899, seen in the photograph on page 43. In 1911 it had been taken over by W Harris, the Cook Shop.

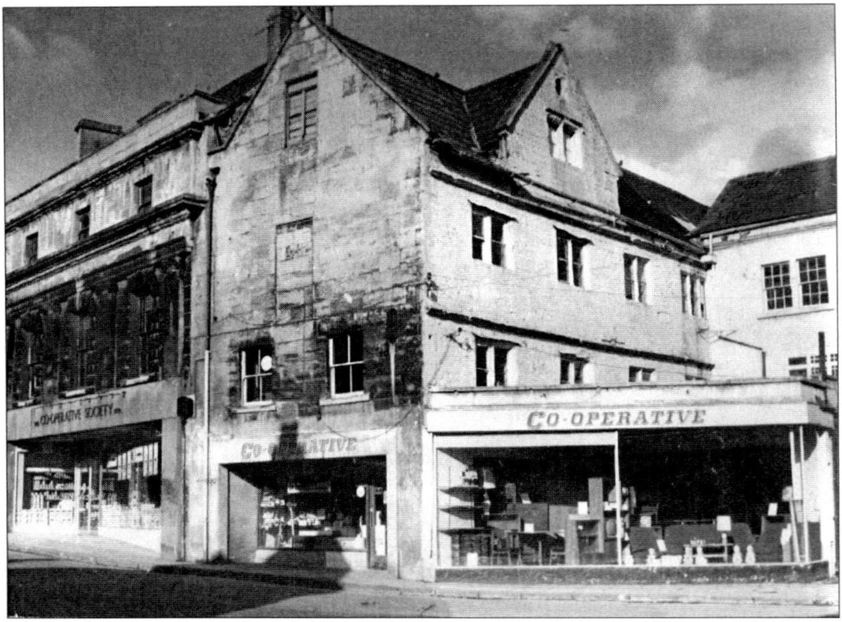

From left to right, the Co-op Grocers, Sweet Shop and Furniture Department, 1968

No. 34 Mrs Durkee's Sweet Shop

In 1952 number 34 was a sweet shop, run initially by Mrs Alice Durkee, then taken over by Mrs White.

> *"She was a dear little old lady in there. I can just see this little old lady looking over the counter, but she was very sweet."* (JS12)

Loose sweets in the early 1950s were sold in 4 ounce (125g) portions, poured from large glass jars into small paper bags – although many children would be coming in here asking for "a pennyworth, please". They'd also be returning empty bottles of Tizer or lemonade to claim their 3 pence refund.

> *"A tube of pastilles or Rowntrees Fruit Gums would be threepence and a pack of Rolos, they'd be sixpence. A packet of nice crayons with papers on, I think they were sixpence. It doesn't sound much now but sixpence, oo, if you had sixpence you were rich! And two shillings and sixpence was even better!"* (AB12)

The shop was a pork butcher from 1885 to 1931. The old cash register used by Benjamin Edwards in 1891 is now on display in the Bradford on Avon Museum. The shop was sold to the Co-op in 1931 for £3,000.

No. 33 The Co-operative Grocers

You can easily identify where the Co-op Grocers was in Silver Street; the original mosaic sign is still there on the pavement outside number 33.

In 1952 this was considered the heart of Bradford on Avon: a busy shop with people bustling in and out with food coupons and shopping baskets. Rationing didn't end until 1954 and queuing was common. The Co-op opened three new shops in Bradford in 1931, this one and a butchers and drapers in the Shambles. The large shop window was installed at this time, desecrating what had been a fine Georgian façade.

> *"You used to have your Co-op divvy number, didn't you, I can always remember what mother had, it was 1606. If we went and did any shopping for mother we always had to remember her divvy number. It was quite an important thing otherwise you felt you were missing out!"* (CB12)

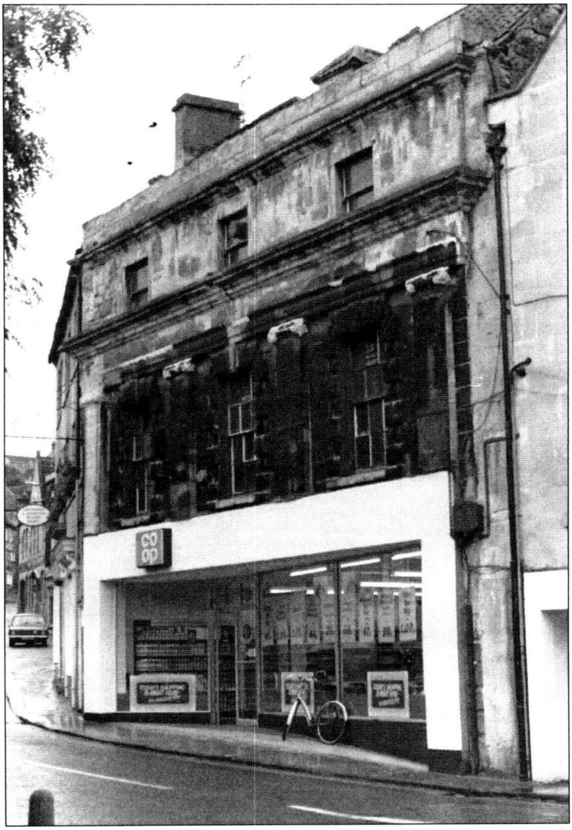

Co-op Grocers in 1987, with a new sign on the façade.
The window ads show Heinz Beans at a shilling and a penny (5p) and Typhoo Tea at 1 shilling and 5½ pence (7p).

"They sold lovely cream horns. My mum used to go down on a Friday – cakes on right, groceries on left, cheese and bacon and cold meats beyond the cakes." (JS12)

Jean Howell (née Webley) recalls her father Harry, a Co-op rep, visiting the outlying villages on his motorbike to take orders which were delivered the following week.[42]

"I think one of the great shames – old fashioned of me – was to see the Co-op disappear. Simply because it was like a little honeycomb. People buzzed in and out and it was a centre." (GS97)[43]

The shop finally closed in 1988 and remained empty for two years before it was restored by Alan and Jenny Hinds from 1990 onwards. The upper part of the building to the rear of the site had been colonised by pigeons and underneath the layers of droppings they discovered further layers of animal fat, a likely connection to the time when it was occupied by a pork butchers. The Hinds discovered a stack of promotional Christmas brochures dating back to the butchers in 1896 and all the old Co-op ledgers and ration records.[44]

The premises were previously occupied by grocers, ironmongers, bootmakers and, out the back, a ropeyard. One of the earliest references to the shops in Bradford shows a linen draper here in 1749. It was also the site of one of the longest established grocers in Bradford, the Budgett Jones dynasty which occupied this site from 1775 to 1899.

No. 32 Bolloms Cleaners and Dyers

In 1952 a trade directory lists Bolloms as operating from number 32.

"You'd have taken your suits there to be cleaned because you had a laundry man call to your door to pick up your laundry." (CB12)

It was occupied later from 1958 to 1965 by Mrs Wiltshire, who moved here from The Chocolate Box, her small sweet shop at the bottom of Market Street.

"She moved up in the world when she moved to Silver Street. She let two or three flats above. That's where she had that fire. She used to keep an awful lot of stock, I suppose they did in those days, they didn't have sell by dates. All sorts of Mars Bars and things like that. But she did have a fire there and everything was melted." (WS12)

No doubt the local children turned up in droves, hoping to scavenge a few reject Mars Bars which in those days cost fourpence (2p) each.

By 1885 James Budgett's young nephew Robert had expanded the family grocery business from next door into three buildings, later selling china and glassware from these premises. This was considered a very smart row of shops by the late nineteenth century. From 1900 to 1926 it was the premises of Joseph Frisby, Boot and Shoe Retailers.

→ Look for ... the old step into the shop, worn away over the years by a steady stream of customers ←

Nos. 30 & 31 J Alex Brown Ironmongers

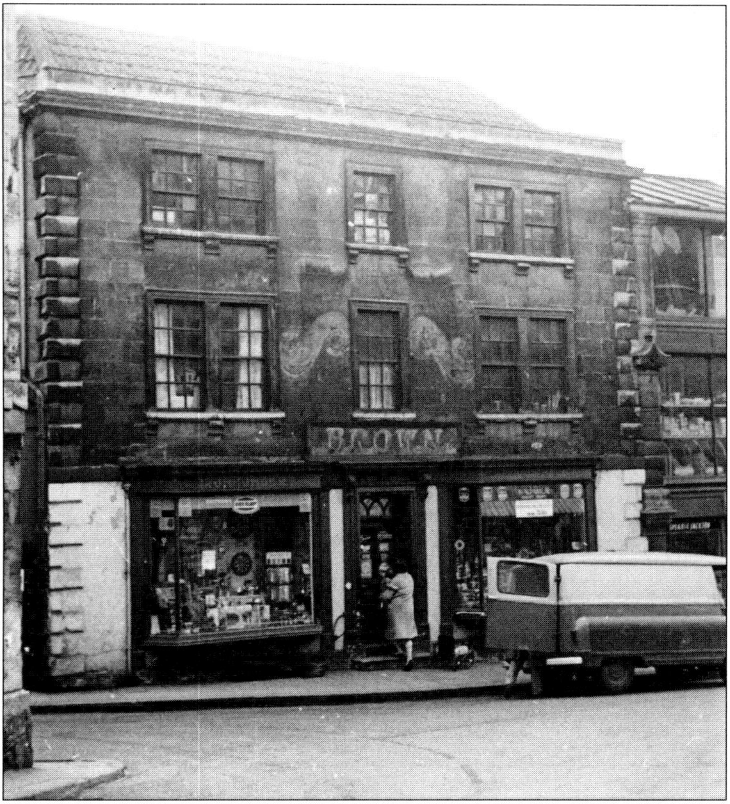

In 1952 J Alex Brown Ironmongers occupied both the existing shop and the charity shop premises next door. Even then it had been trading for almost a hundred years. It was founded in 1853 by John Brown and his son John Alexander took over when he died, installing a workshop in an old weaving shed up Coppice Hill over the road. Subsequent owners retained the name, including Hugh Holloway who ran it in 1952.

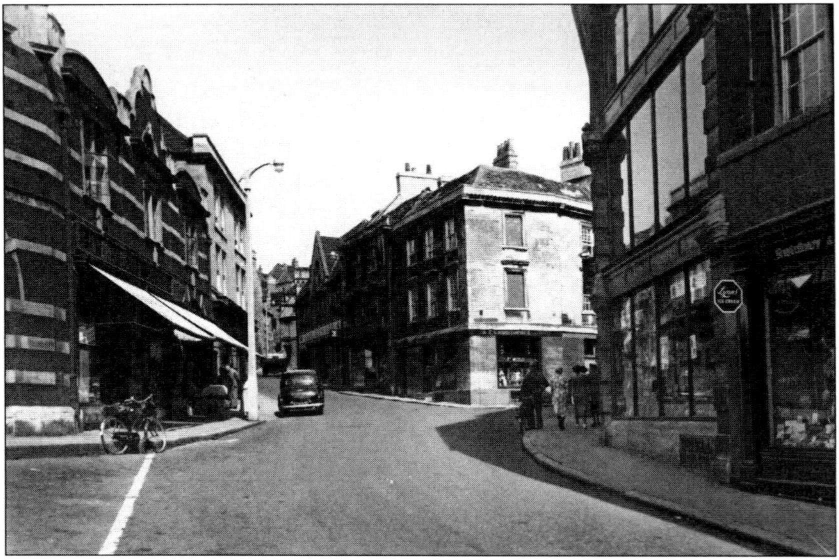

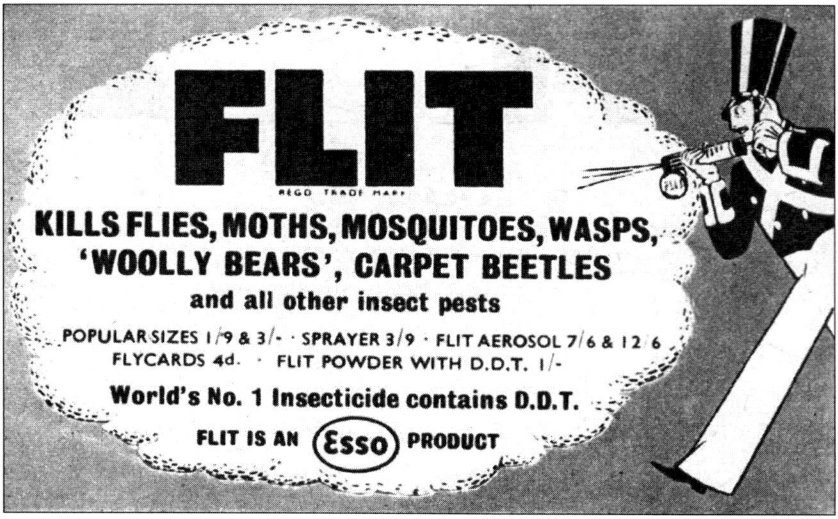

In the Fifties, washing powder was typically about one shilling (5p) a box, toilet paper was invariably the hard pine-smelling variety and although light bulbs were fast taking over, hardware shops still sold quantities of gas mantles. Many homes were without inside bathrooms, a situation which was changing by the end of the decade.

"Very much old-fashioned, they sold paint and bits and pieces. It went down as far as the charity shop but you never went down there – that was more or less their storage place. Most of it was derelict, I think. They stored up on the first floor as well." (CB12)

Back in the 19th century, business was booming. In 1860 John Brown expanded into the premises next door, known as Number 2 showrooms and advertised with a large kettle perched on the chimney top. In 1867 he demolished the rather cramped showrooms and replaced them with imposing glass fronted premises.

The business suffered from competition from large DIY stores towards the end of the 20th century, losing the showrooms and the upper floors which were converted to flats.

→ **Look for . . . the old shop sign painted high on the front wall** ←

No. 29 Christopher's Chemist

In 1952 this old established shop at number 29 was still going strong almost fifty years after it opened in 1908. Richard Christopher ran it until his death in 1962, when his daughter, Miss Angela, continued the business. It finally closed in 1986 and residents of the town succeeded in saving the shop interior and contents, hardly changed since the turn of the century. They're now installed in their entirety in the Bradford on Avon Museum. Miss Angela was a fondly-remembered sympathetic soul.

"If you had a headache she would give you an aspirin and a glass of water." (WS12)

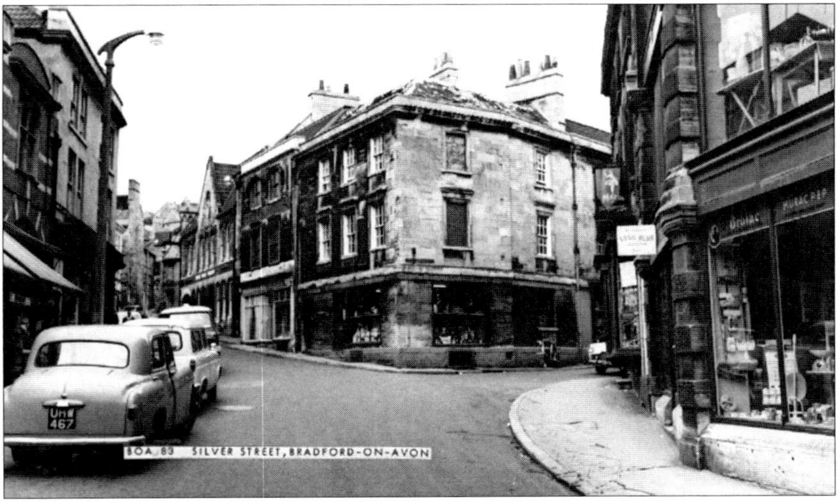

Mr Christopher spent some time in Singapore and India after he qualified as a pharmacist and as soon as he was established in Silver Street he began work on a range of perfumes and cosmetics inspired by his travels, advertised in the local town directory in 1911.

> *"The New Indian Perfume Siva. A perfect blending of Oriental Odours. Reminding one of the seductive fragrance of a Floral Festival in the Temples of the Far East. Prices from 10½ d to 5/- ."*

> *"He made curry powder and Siva, the perfume. But the scent was awful, wasn't it?! But we only had Parma Violets in those days, and Yardley's Lavender and Chanel, I suppose. There wasn't a lot of choice."* (WS12)

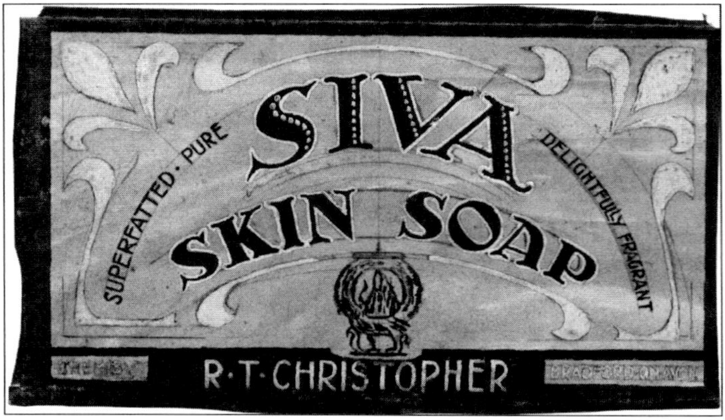

Mr Christopher's own hand-drawn design for Siva Soap

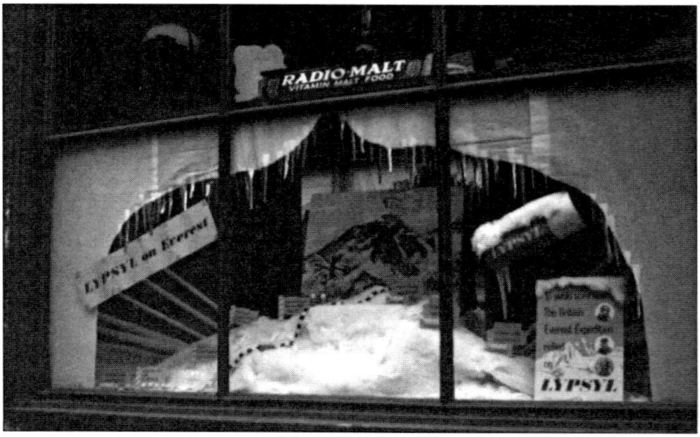

Christopher's window celebrates the vital role played by Lypsyl in the 1953 Everest ascent

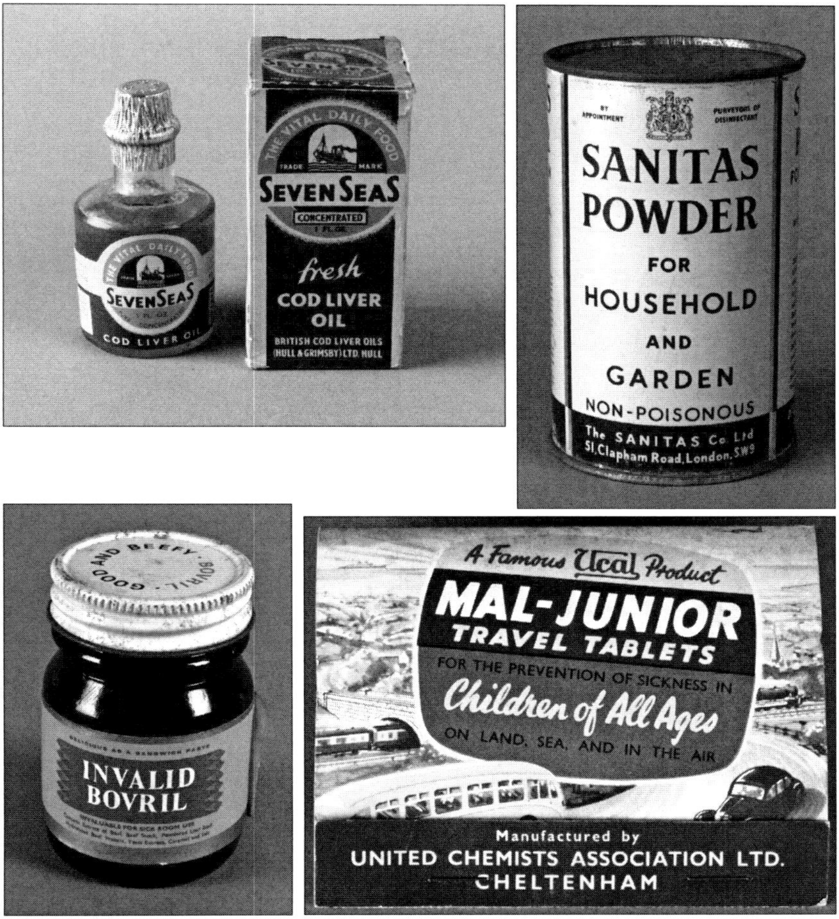

Selection of goods from Christopher's Chemists

Another resident remembers a different range of products:

> *"You could buy things and get up to all sorts of mischief in those days, explosions and the like!"* (RS12)

There had been a chemist on this site from 1863 when Thomas Prideaux Saunders first set up shop. It continued as a chemist until 1908 when it was sold to Richard Christopher. A keen historian, he saved many of the antiquarian features and products of the shop, to the great benefit of Museum visitors where they may be seen in a fascinating reconstruction of the pharmacy.

No. 28 Henry Rowe Photographer

In 1952 these premises, now an estate agent, were occupied by two businesses: Henry Rowe Photographer on the left side and a hairdressers named Taviner and Dobson on the right.

The photographers developed into a television rental business, a branch of Rediffusion, but earlier in its life, the shop housed a succession of printing works beginning in 1881 with George Farrington, then Dotesio and Todd around 1900. The shop also representated a telephone company. They couldn't have had much trade. Despite being invented in 1876, by the early 1950s only 10% of the population had a 'phone.

→ **Look for . . . "Printing Office" high up on the front wall of the shop** ←

No. 27 Dodge's Shoe Shop

In 1952 the Chinese takeaway was an offshoot of Mark Uncles' Shoe Shop in Market Street. A bootmaker had been in these premises from at least 1911.

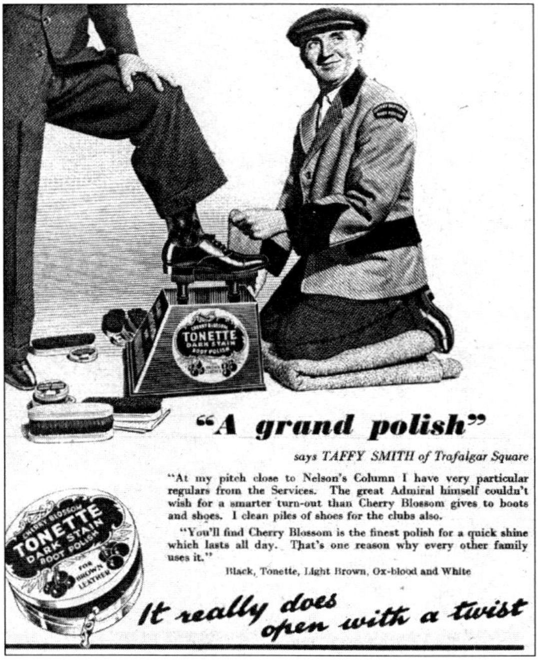

→ **Look for ... the boot scraper by the door, set unfeasibly close to the wall** ←

~ The next shop is some distance further up the road and can best be seen from the pavement opposite ~

No. 24 Bowyers Builders

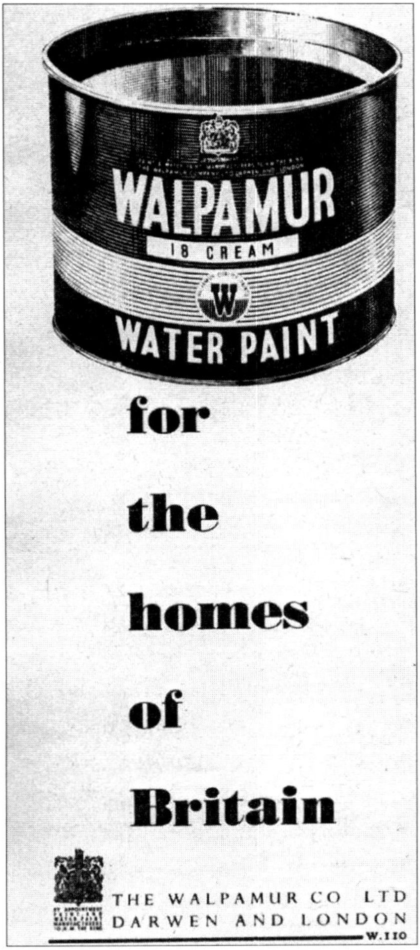

In 1952 Bowyers Builders had premises in this handsome building with the elaborate façade. A long established family in Bradford on Avon, Bowyers is still a local business, now a funeral directors in the Bull Pit.

"We had that as a DIY shop. We sold paint, timber, wallpaper. Father opened it up just about 1952 or a couple of years after. Mainly it was painters and decorators who did it but the trend of DIY was just beginning to happen and as we were builders, people started to come in and buy stuff to do their own bits and pieces. They come to buy a piece of timber so then father opened up a shop, but he didn't get going like Focus and B&Q, he should have got onto that bandwagon!" (CB12)

In the early 1950s there was a shortage of skilled labour and some enterprising homeowners decided to have a go themselves. Little did they anticipate the DIY boom to come. At this time the only paint available for walls was white or magnolia distemper, but by the end of the decade colour had taken off – although restricted to a fairly subdued range of pastels.

Built in the early 1880s when the road was widened, this building was known as The Vaults and used as a store by Taylors Wine Merchants who were over the road where the Bunch of Grapes pub now be found.

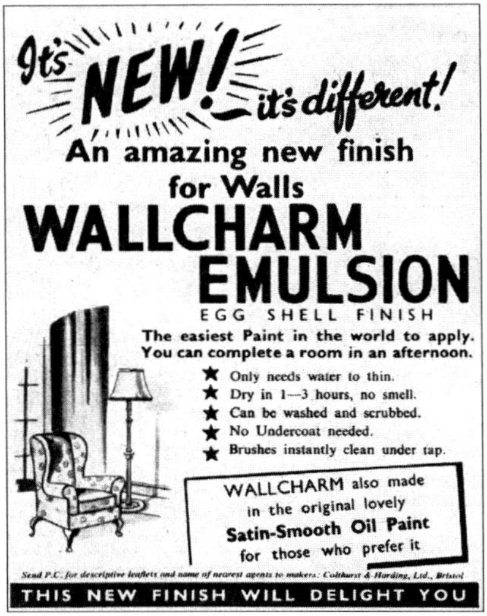

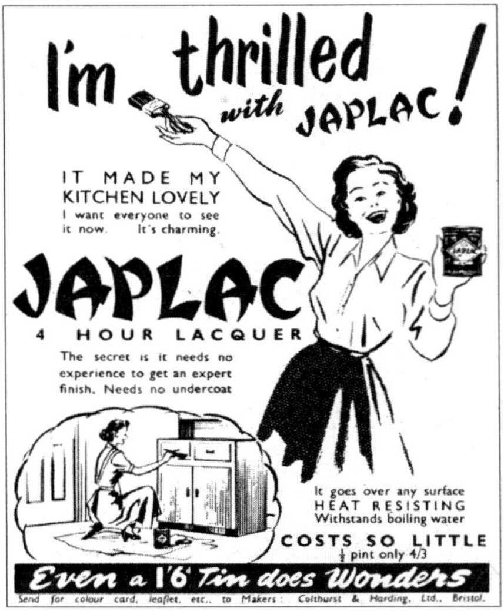

→ Look for ... the carved stone heads of Bacchus, Ariadne and other figures from Greek mythology on the front of the building ←

No. 22 The Silver Fish Saloon

In 1952 Ted Smith ran a popular fish and chip shop in these restaurant premises at 22 Silver Street. He also travelled to the town's outskirts and Winsley in his mobile fish and chip van, as happily still happens today.

There were two other outlets in the town: Mrs Ann's Fish and Chip shop in Market Street and another one along Sladesbrook, known as The Admiral's Cabin.

A former local resident, Bertram Niblett, recalls:

"The proprietor of the fish and chip shop after the First World War cooked fish and chips together in a cauldron over a coal fire. They tasted very good from newspaper. This little shop was two doors up from the present shop in Silver Street and next door to the old cottage."[45]

~ The shops on the north side of Silver Street begin at number 17, further up on the corner of Whitehill ~

No. 17 Teeds Antique Shop

In 1952 John Teed was one of the first of a new influx of antiques dealers settling in the town. He set up business in this shop on the corner of Silver Street and Whitehill and by the 1970s his reputation was so established that Princess Margaret came to call when she visited the area. Bradford on Avon was famous for its antiques shops.

"Increasingly during the late 1970s particularly, and then the early 1980s, various other dealers moved into the town, and it became well known, so if you were out and about, say in the north of England, or in London, and you said you were from Bradford on Avon, people didn't say, 'Oh, that is where the Saxon church is'. They might say 'Oh, that is a lovely old town', but they always said, 'Oh, and all those nice antique shops!'". (AJ11)[46]

This was formerly the antiques shop of two remarkable ladies who played an important role in safeguarding some of Bradford's most historic buildings by founding the Bradford on Avon Preservation Trust. Elizabeth Stephenson and Kathleen MacKean were known as "The China Hens", after the name of their shop. Previously, it was occupied in the 1930s by William Dotesio, Printer.

No. 15 Archards Hairdressers

In 1952 Mr and Mrs Archard were hairdressers here: gents on the left and ladies on the right. They were established for decades and in the early 1950s were one of four hairdressers in the centre of town.

"Mr Alfie Archard, he would only do his regulars towards the end. If anyone came in to him and he said 'Where did you go last time?' and they said, 'Oo, we went down the road', he'd say 'Well, you better get down there now and have it done again!' - but he was very old!" (CB12)

"They used to have those big things then that you used to sit under to curl your hair up on and it was all attached to these wires. You put this big, ugly thing over your head, a massive thing. I don't understand how it worked, it used to look frightening and I know my mother never liked it! She kept her hair long as a rule and did it in a bun! She said it was frightening to sit under it." (JS12)

In 1886 Aaron Smith was busy making and repairing umbrellas in this building. Aaron also doubled as the Monkton Farleigh Postal Messenger – perhaps umbrellas were a subject dear to his heart. It was occupied from 1893 to 1903 by William Hunt, a draper.

At this point in Silver Street a narrow alley heads up to Whitehill. Now known as the Cut, it is thought to derive from Cut Throat Lane – although Canon Jones, the local historian who wrote much about the town, believes it was more likely to be Cut Through Lane, which seems a reasonable and less threatening assumption.[47]

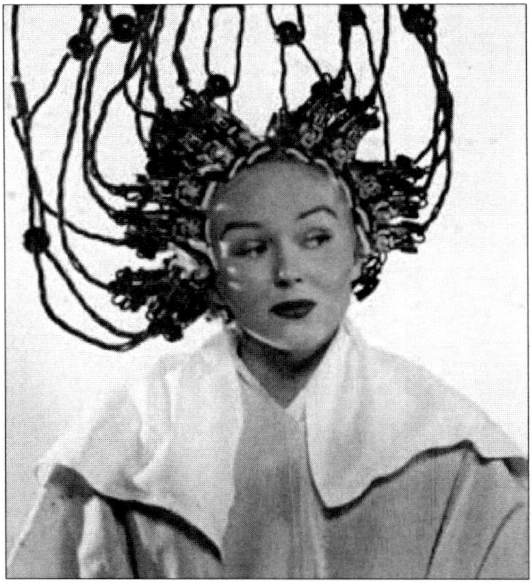

No. 12 Seviour's Grocers

In 1952 Mrs Seviour ran a tiny grocery and dairy here, selling produce that her husband grew in New Road.[48]

In those days people had their milk delivered. The milkman would come round,

> *"with the milk in a big churn and measure out the milk, it was wonderful. He came round with a van and mum would go out with a jug."* (AB12)

Cheese would be cut to order with a wire, wrapped in greaseproof paper, and the price scrawled on it with a pencil which the shopkeeper kept behind his ear.

In 1886 there was a Juvenile Tailor and Hatter at work here but it was J Stevens Dairy by 1903. When betting was legalised in 1961, this was the first bookies in Wiltshire, opened by Mr John Banks, Senior in the early 1960s.

No. 11 Giddings Grocers

In 1952 this grocers was in strong competition with the 'better class' Nichols & Bushell of Market Street, not to mention the International Stores further down Silver Street and the Co-op Grocers near the bridge. Oh, and Mrs Seviour's Grocers next door at number 12!

"There were many more shops in those days because people could find employment within Bradford on Avon. Avon Rubber was the main employer but there were other small factories like Dotesio's (printers) and Weir Electrical." (AB12)

"You used to go shopping once or twice a day. Even if you lived up the top of the hill, you'd walk down to the shops at least once a day." CB of BOA

In the 1952 housewife's basket would be a quarter of corned beef for 1 shilling, a bottle of Camp Coffee with chicory (only 4% coffee) – but no tea bags. They didn't come in until 1953 when they were regarded as a tremendous novelty.

This shop is believed to contain part of one of the oldest domestic buildings in Bradford on Avon, dating back to the 15th century. It has a long history of grocery selling. In 1882 it was James Gore's Grocers and later the Silver Street Dairy where Mr Stevens sold milk in 1918 for a penny a glass.

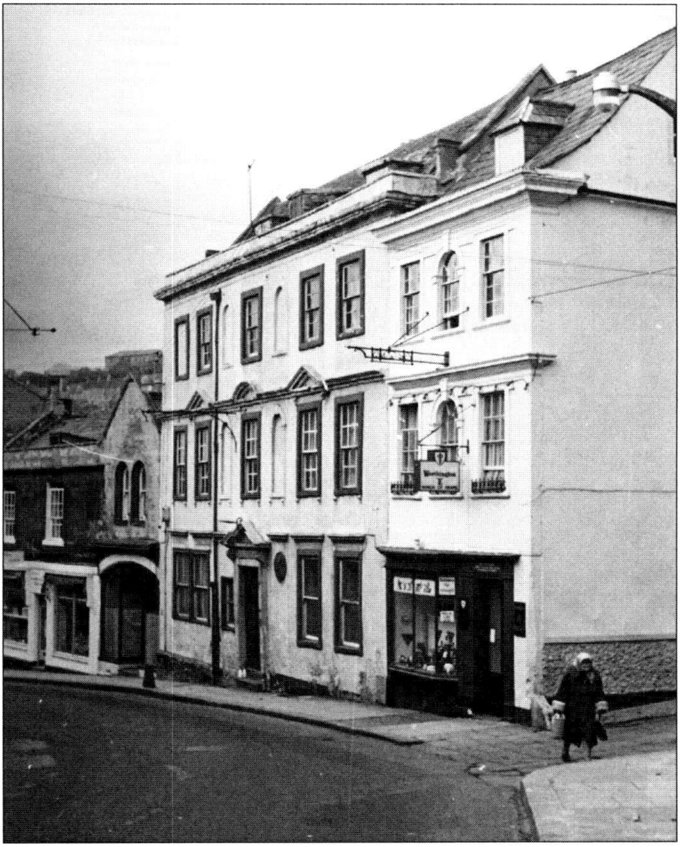

No. 10 Harold Windo Butchers

In 1952 this was either Harold Windo Butchers or A T Scrine Butchers. Local residents are divided on this and the local trade directory is also unclear. There has been a butcher's shop on this site for over 180 years, since at least 1830 and the building is known as Canterbury House thanks to its supply of New Zealand Lamb over a century ago. The 1911 local trade directory advised: 'Try our Canterbury Lamb. It is acknowledged as one of the luxuries of the present day.'

Animals were fetched from the market and driven up the nearby alley to a slaughterhouse at the back.

> *"I can remember a couple of cows being pushed up the alleyway . . . They killed cattle up there behind the butcher's shop and then hung the fresh meat straightaway." (EW89)* [49]

Mrs Holbrook, born Lily Banks in 1909, remembers peeping from the bedroom window:

> *". . . we used to watch the cows being killed. They used to chop them down through the head. There was a big place where the blood used to collect down this slope and a great big sink with a tap. Weren't we bloodthirsty girls, though!" (LH97)* [50]

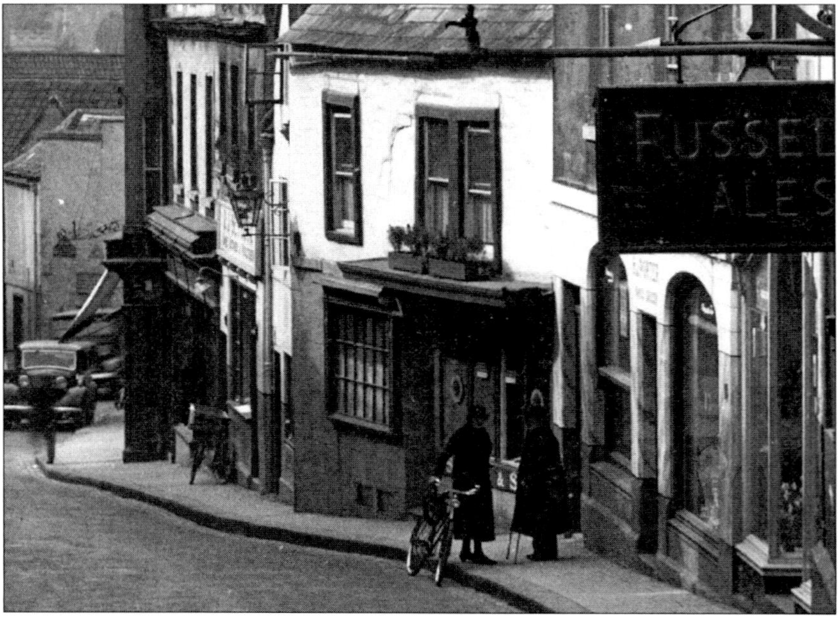

Robert Seymour and family ran their butchers' shop here from 1903 until 1920, when they moved next door. They were renowned for their extravagant displays of produce hanging outside the shop on high days and holidays. Great sides of beef and pork were draped in evergreens and lit by paraffin lights.

→ Look for . . . the original ceiling rails where the joints of meat were suspended and the old window fixings, allowing the shop to be opened up to the street ←

No. 9 O R Johns Butchers

In 1952 this little sweet shop was occupied by the butcher, O R Johns. The competition was close by – there was another butcher right next door at number 10, in addition to a further three in the centre of town.

In the 50s a major challenge for housewives was keeping the meat fresh.

"Meat was a bit of problem to keep when you had it on Friday for the weekend. Our larder had open vents at the side and if you put your meat in there, even if you covered it with gauze, the flies would get through and lay their eggs on the meat and if you weren't careful you'd certainly find maggots in there and you'd have to wash it with vinegar. In the end I took to putting the fresh meat in my oven! We were all electric and as long as I wasn't using my oven, that was the coolest place to put it!" (JH09)

In 1886 it was occupied by Mrs Ellen Cabell's Confectioners and by 1911 it was a grocers. In 1920 Robert Seymour the butcher moved in from number 10 next door and stayed here until 1949.

The narrow shop at 9a was home to Ernie Sadd's barber shop for many years after he moved here from his salon upstairs in the Town Hall where he was based in 1952.

→ Explore the narrow alleyway alongside which led to the abattoir around the back. You can still see the grooves made by the cattle horns as they were herded along to their doom ←

Nos. 7 & 8 Goodalls Drapers and Outfitters

In 1952 the two shops at numbers 7 and 8 (the Indian take away) were occupied by J F Goodall, Drapers and Outfitters, run by Harold Rowlandson who retained the shop's original name. This was a much loved and rather old-fashioned shop, whose stock hardly changed from the Fifties through to the Nineties when it finally closed. The last incumbent, Frank Goodall, was very chuffed to acquire a business which quite co-incidentally bore his name! Goodalls carried a fascinating range of haberdashery including repair kits for stockings and discreet little devices made from tiny silk loops and safety pins to hold a multitude of shoulder straps together.

> *"It was lovely in there. A drapery shop where you could buy dress material and wool and haberdashery. And next to that was a men's outfitting shop with a very nice man in there. I remember going in to buy my father's Christmas present and in those days you didn't have many pennies to spend but they treated you as if you were a grown up, it was lovely!"* (AB12)

> *"They sold the green and purple gingham for the Fitzmaurice Grammar School for the girls."* (JS12)

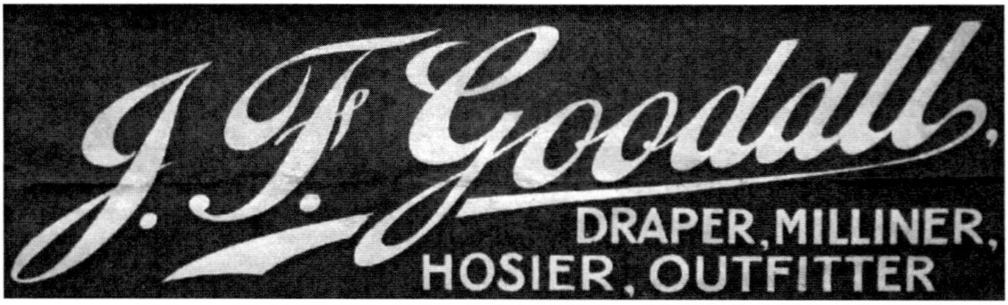

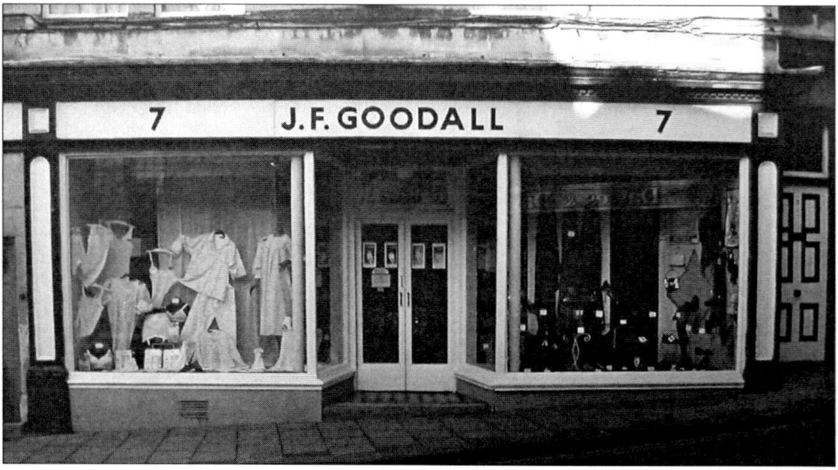

Goodalls in the 1990s, relatively unchanged since the 1950s

Although clothes rationing ended in 1949, the 'make do and mend' culture persisted into the 1950s with people altering or making their own. Since then, increased spending power and less home time has seen the sad decline of haberdashers such as Goodalls.

The shop has long been connected with clothing, from 1822 when it was occupied by John Alford, linen draper, and in 1876 William Rogers, a silk mercer and undertaker who had the façade restyled. John Frank Goodall bought it in the 1890s and the drapers continued in business here for over a century. A display in the Bradford on Avon Museum gives a flavour of the period habadashery on sale.

No. 6a Scrine's Chemists

In 1952 this small shop was Arnold Scrine the Chemists. He was related to the family of butchers who had a shop up the road but trained with Richard Christopher, the popular chemist on the other side of Silver Street. He set up his own business here at least as early as 1925. After his death at the early age of 47 in 1958 the shop continued with new owners still trading under the name of Arnold Scrine until the year 2000.

These are the only brick buildings in the centre of town. Built in Edwardian times to house Harding's Brewery, they replaced old medieval buildings which on this part of the site were occupied by pork butchers from 1867 to 1899.

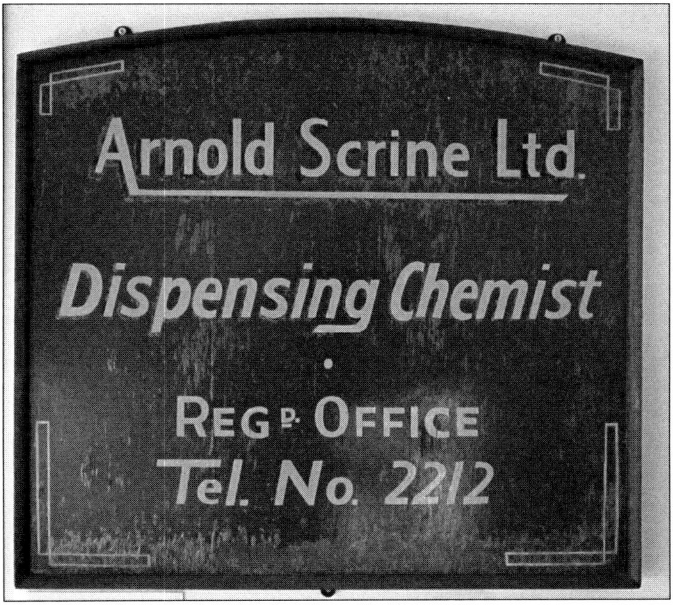

No. 6 International Stores

In 1952 the International Stores handled many of the food ration coupons issued in the town. Food rationing didn't end until 1954.

A resident of Bradford on Avon who worked in the shop in the Fifties remembers it well.

> *"The rations back then included ½lb of bacon, 4oz of butter, 1lb of sugar, 2 eggs per person per week - and ½lb of tea to last the month. It all had to be weighed out and counted up – all in shillings and pence then and you did it in your head as you went. A pork pie cost 9 pence!"* (RC12)

> *"The shop goes right back under arches, under Coppice Hill. We used it for storage. We kept seed potatoes in the far one, dark and cold. I left to run the stores at Avon Rubber. First week I went down there, I earned double what I'd been getting! I was twenty then. I didn't want to be working 'til 6 o'clock on Saturday night."* (RC12)

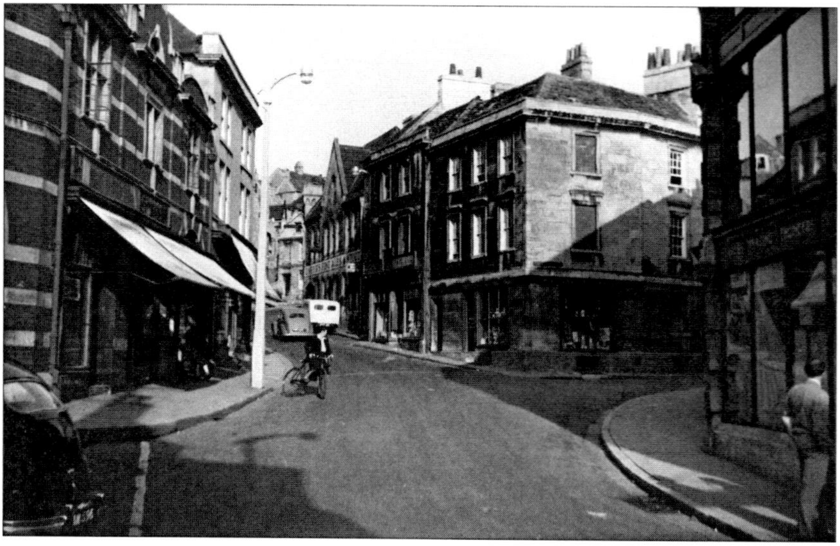

The new brick buildings were constructed in 1899 for Harding's Brewery. Harding's was almost immediately bought by Ruddles, who were there until 1910. The middle arch was the entrance to the loading bay in the brewery yard behind.

Bertram Niblett recalls,

> *"I can remember seeing the beer and ale steaming away in the boilers, and the horsedrawn drays pulling up Silver Street, laden with barrels. The horses backed the*

drays into the loading bay . . . The steps in the far right-hand corner of the chemist shop are where the actual loading bay was."[51]

The old buildings formerly on this site housed a succession of hatters, tailors and outfitters at the end of the nineteenth century.

When Ruddles Brewery moved out in 1910 the building housed the first of several grocers on this site, including Thomas Coupland in the 1930s.

→ Look for . . . the Harding's Brewery sign over the left and middle arches, under the awnings. Up Coppice Hill alongside the King's Arms and on the right is the entrance to the old brewery yard where the remains of the brewery chimney can still be seen ←

No. 4 The King's Arms

In 1952 the off licence at number 4 was part of the King's Arms, with a bottle of whisky costing £1.15s. (£1.75). The pub survived on this site since at least 1809 until its closure and eventual conversion to residential use in 2013. There was an earlier tavern here for centuries in what was then the old Market Place occupying this open space alongside The Shambles.

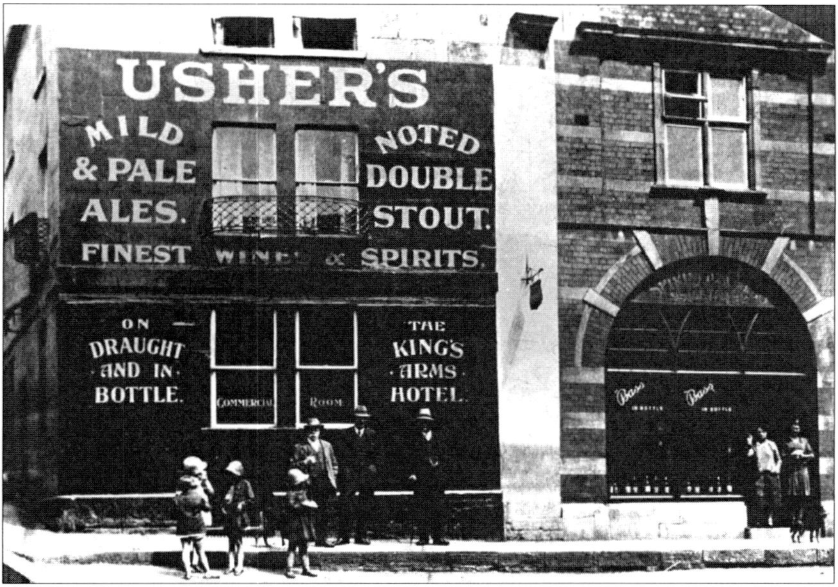

The King's Arms, Silver Street, c. 1930

~ Silver Street continues past the end of the Shambles, down the hill towards the bridge and crosses the bottom of Market Street ~

No. 3 The Chocolate Box

This small shop on the corner of Silver Street and Market Street was Mrs Wiltshire's sweet shop where she also sold bread.

> *"She was a lovely old soul, a little bit untidy, but she'd sell the bread and on bank holidays the queues would come out of her shop and all the way half way across the town bridge. She was the busiest in that little shop before she moved across to Silver Street. She always used to, if the chocolates didn't work out to be a quarter, she used to cut them in half! They didn't have that many sweets, boiled sweets, toffees in glass jars."* (CB12)

> *"She wore knitted fingerless gloves in the winter."* (AB12)

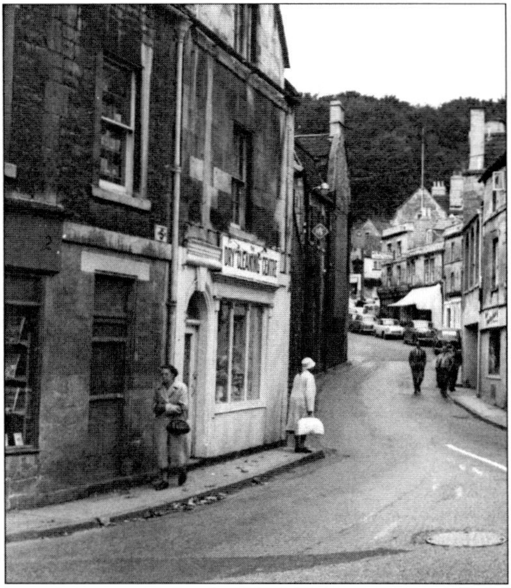

In 1886 this was A Alexander, Tailor, in 1893 S E Haynes milliner and draper and in 1897 Albert Scrine's English and Colonial Meat Company, with a beautiful glass lantern suspended on a curved bracket hanging above the door. That must have been an early casualty when big lorries started coming through. By 1960, the approximate date of the photograph, it was the Dry Cleaning Centre.

Nos. 1 & 2 Ward's Stationers and Newsagents

This is still referred to as Ward's Corner, after Atkinson Ward who was here in 1952 running a stationers and newsagents. His wife was the well-known writer Fay Infawn. Originally one shop it is now divided in two with a sandwich shop next to the entrance to the Swan Hotel, and just opened in 2013, a tattoo parlour alongside.

"You went into the place on the left to buy your newspapers, then up a little ramp into next door on the right where they used to sell all the stationery and then upstairs and see all the toys on the first floor. That was the main place for toys in Bradford. I used to like the Dinky Cars and every time they bought a new model out they used to tell us. And Meccano with nuts and bolts, no clipping things together then!" (CB12)

"They had a lovely toy shop and all the farmyard animals were set out and we'd go in there with our pocket money and buy a cow or a pig and make a collection ourselves." (AB12)

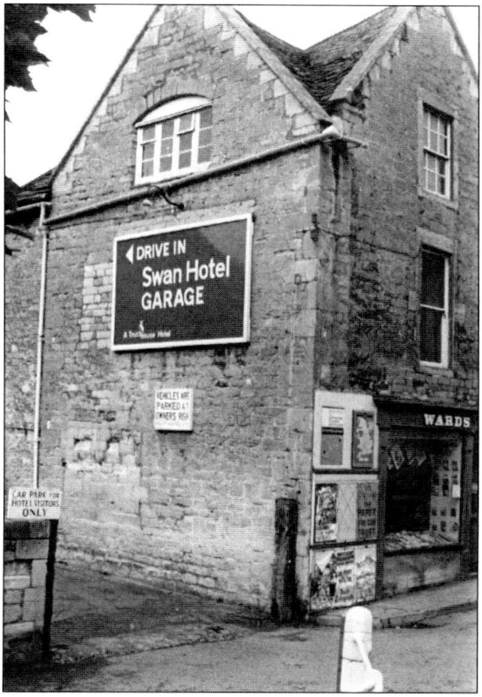

In 1952 most toys were 'Made in Britain' and pocket money was diligently saved for the latest Dinky Car, costing about 5 shillings. Dolls were frequently made of 'composition', a mix of cardboard and papier maché, before being painted. Plastic, considered a new wonder material, was common by the end of the decade.

Early residents in number 1 were Isaac Few, Shopkeeper, in 1867 and 1886 and the Misses Emily and Alice Merrett had a stationery shop here from 1899 to 1911.

Number 2 housed George Gore, boot and shoe maker in 1886 and later, from 1891 to 1920, it was Mark Uncles' first shoe shop.

~ Walking past the rear entrance to the Swan Hotel, the short road alongside the river passes the site of the Bull Pit, the site of bull baiting with dogs in the eighteenth century. The Street Trail continues up Hang Dog Alley where Lydia Rudman ran her Coffee Tavern on the right-hand side. Popular with the local millworkers, it was demolished in 1950 ~

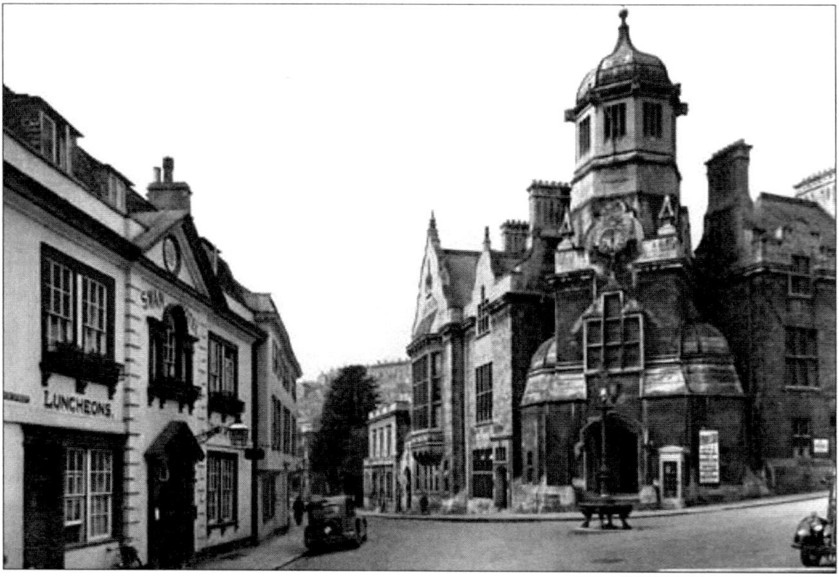

Church Street

In the late 14th century, we know that Church Street led to the lay courthouse and

> *"At the gate of the court were four shops and the manorial bakers, also the court pigeon house."*[52]

In the eighteenth and nineteenth centuries it would have thronged with crowds enjoying the Bradford fair which stretched along Church Street and into Market Street. Daniel Batchelor recalls a memory from around 1835 in a letter to the local paper:

> *"Bradford fair too is gone, they say. When I was a devourer of gingerbread, the stalls laden with that refection extended from the Swan Inn to Edmond's factory in Church Street, and nearly up to the 'baish' on Pippet street."*[53]

In the 1950s, Church Street would have bustled with factory workers heading for Abbey Mill. Owned by Spencer Moulton, it was the world's biggest supplier of small rubber gaskets for sealing aerosol cans, producing millions annually until the factory closed in the 1990s. Like other former mill buildings in the town, it has since been converted into housing.

~ Turning left along Church Street, number 6 is two doors down ~

No. 6 Eileen's, Ladies Hairdresser

In 1952 number 6, as today, was also a hairdressers, then run by Miss Eileen Turner. It was considered the most upmarket of the Bradford hairdressers. One older resident of the town remembers his mother did not feel comfortable there.

> *"No, too posh. She went to Maison Beryl. She couldn't possibly have gone in there 'cos it was much too posh for her. There was a lot of that in Bradford in those days, you know, sort of like upper crust you know. My father was only a rubber factory worker you see – so you see there would have maybe been sort of a class distinction there."* (JB12)

In 1844 it was occupied by Aaron Bishop, baker, and in 1891 by George Beasley, watchmaker and jeweller.

~ The Street Trail doubles back along Church Street towards Market Street ~

No. 5 J S Green, Gents Outfitters

In 1952 Jesse Green was running a Gentleman's Outfitters at number 5, now a florist, with his wife Dora and son Reginald. In the early Fifties, casual dress for chaps was sports jackets and flannels and it was still the norm to wear trilbies or caps. The rite of passage from boy to man was marked by a visit to the outfitters to be measured for your first suit. Styles were moving away from the high-waisted, full-trousered, double-breasted suit, with braces for trousers and socks – to a leaner, single-breasted profile. Schoolboys still wore caps and shorts into their early teens.

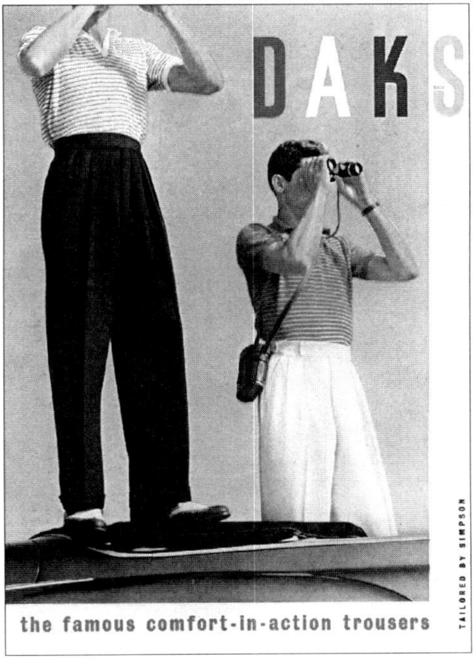

From 1886 to 1910 this was the home of Roland Hendy, Saddler and Harness maker, close to Holy Trinity Church where he was the church organist.

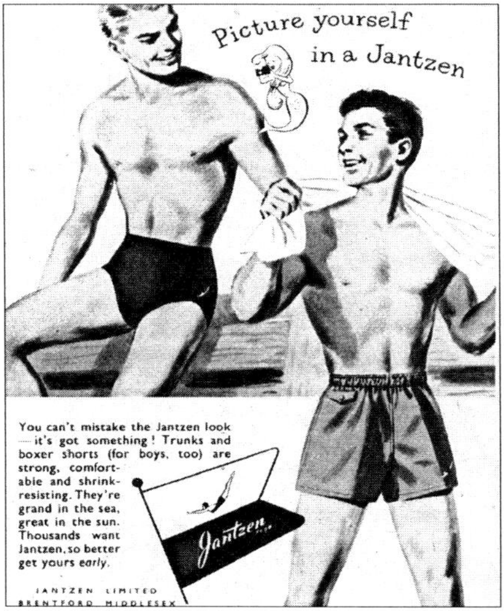

No. 4 Private house

In 1952 this was a private house. From 1896 to 1911 it was occupied by James Rudman, a boot and shoe maker, and his wife Ellen Maria, a dressmaker. The Rudmans were well established in the town. Lydia Rudman ran the Coffee Tavern in Hang Dog Alley around the corner; Frank Rudman was a bootmaker in Market Street; Cornelius Rudman, a Tailor and China Dealer in the Shambles and, back in 1848, Joseph Rudman was a tailor in Newtown.

A boot and shoe maker is listed as working in Church Street in 1830, and by 1848 there were three in this road alone at a time when the cloth trade was in serious decline in the town.

No. 3 Veater's Dairy

In 1952 this solicitor's office was Veater's Dairy, an essential shop at a time when most homes lacked a 'fridge and dairy products were frequently bought or delivered daily.

CB, who lived in the same street, recalls:

"They'd go in there for their milk, their butter, cheese and everything like that. Very old fashioned, just one counter. Old Mrs Veater used to work behind the counter and her husband and their son Len would deliver the milk with an old car with a

trailer on the back. It used to be delivered in churns by the farmer to the dairy which was down the bottom of the garden here. There was a cold place down there. They had flagstones on the floor. They used to deliver it out of the churns and leave it in the jugs on the doorstep." (CB12)

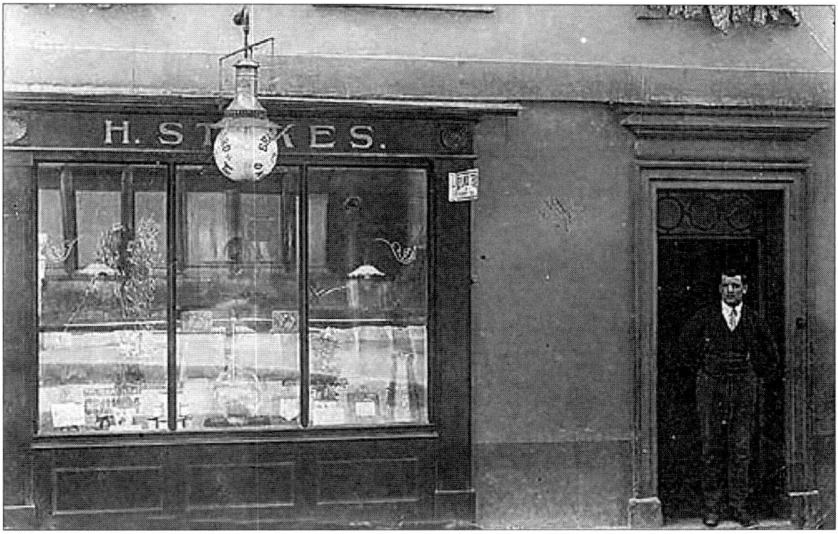

Harry Stokes, proprietor of the Bradford Dairy, 1909

It had been a dairy with various owners since at least 1899, and was known as the Bradford Dairy, run by Harry Stokes, from at least 1905 to 1916. Before then it was a pawnbroker, with a listing in the local directory from 1848.

~ The Street Trail crosses the road to the Roman Catholic Church, the imposing building on the corner of Church Street and Market Street ~

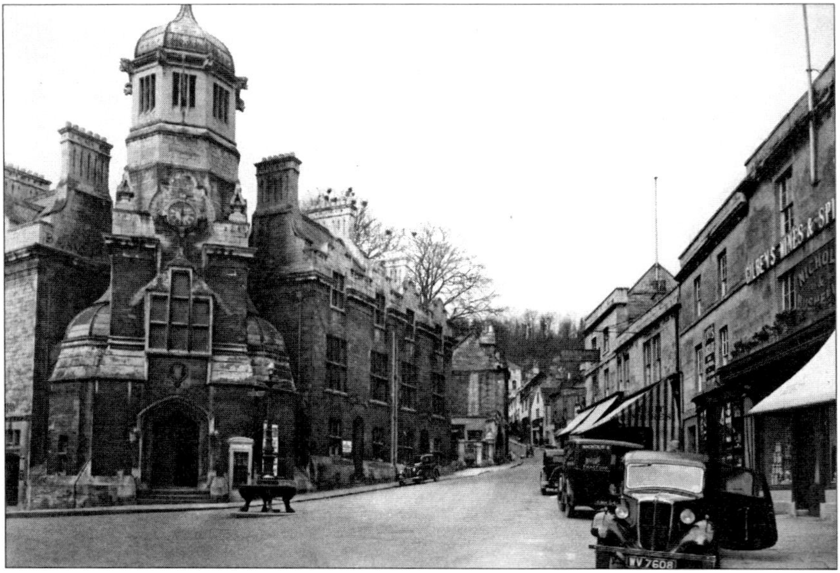

Market Street

Originally called Pippet Street, with records of this name as far back as 1583,[54] the road was renamed when the town market moved here in 1841 from Silver Street. The narrow section at the bottom end of the road was once known as Horse Street, with reference to an old word meaning "muddy", although the Victorian local historian Canon Jones claimed it was named after an old inn called The Scribbling Horse, possibly on the corner of The Shambles and Market Street.[55]

The annual June fair was held here from medieval times[56], where cattle, horses and goods were bought and sold and servants hired, but this tradition had ended by 1907.[57]

Nowadays how many people walking past the Catholic Church in the old Town Hall have any idea that it was once the town cinema? Built on the site of the New Market Tavern, the Town Hall opened in 1855. It housed the Council Offices until 1910 when it became the venue for the first silent films shown in Bradford. Between 1911 and 1920 the picture house was run by Mr Keen, with accompaniment from a lady pianist, and it was still going strong in the 1950s.

The photograph on page 75 was taken the week they were showing such comedy gems as *Midnight Escape* with Stanley Holloway and *Take me to Paris* with Albert Modley, which establishes the year as 1950. Films were advertised on boards propped outside on the pavement and tickets cost one shilling and sixpence (8p).

As was common in the 1950s the streets were devoid of traffic – and road markings. It's illuminating to compare this photo with the current view of Market Street crammed with zigzags, hatching and double yellow lines – and also interesting to note that this same section of Market Street will once again feel like a calmer place when the proposed shared space scheme is installed.[58]

The Post Office Telephones van in the photo might well be there to service the telephone or empty the box of coins; just two old pennies to make a call in the days of 'Press Button B'. But how many of the town's youth knew the trick of wangling a free call by depressing the cradle to mimic the dialling clicks, a technique which required some skill.

Unusually, the cinema also accommodated a barber. The board on the steps announces 'R F Whiting, Gentlemen's High Class Hairdressers, upstairs turn right'. By 1952 there were two hairdressers installed upstairs.

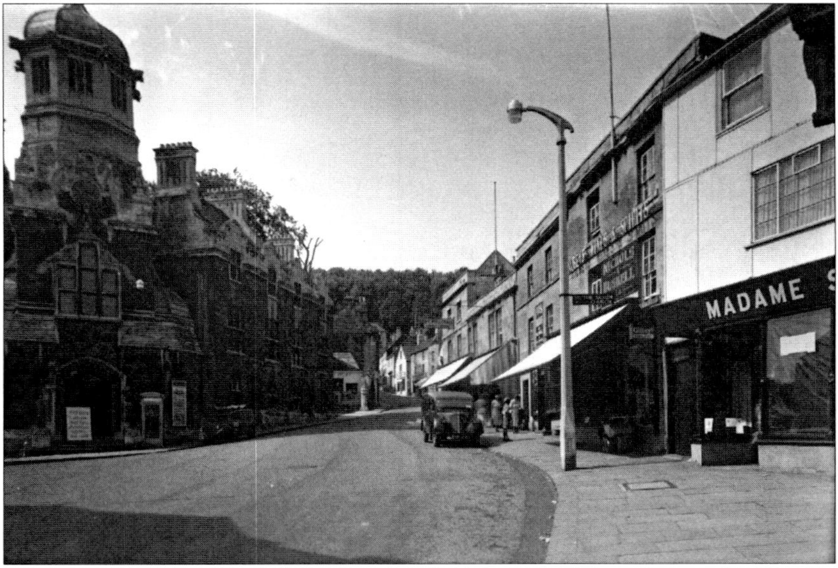

No. 3 Ernie Sadd Hairdressers

In 1952 Ernie Sadd was cutting hair on the first floor of today's Catholic Church.

"It was quite a relief when Mr Sadd came to town because he seemed a little more

human than the others! It was just straight up before then, short as you could right up to the top with a tuft - and Mr Sadd gave us a bit of style. We had Brylcreem with Mr Sadd, or Vitalis. You could have a little wave with it. It was the place you went to have a bit of a better haircut rather than the usual straight back and sides." (CB12)

Tubs of Brylcreem started at one shilling and eightpence (8p). Ever-ready blades were advertised to banish five o'clock shadow with 'a super cutting edge only 1/15th the thickness of cigarette paper.'

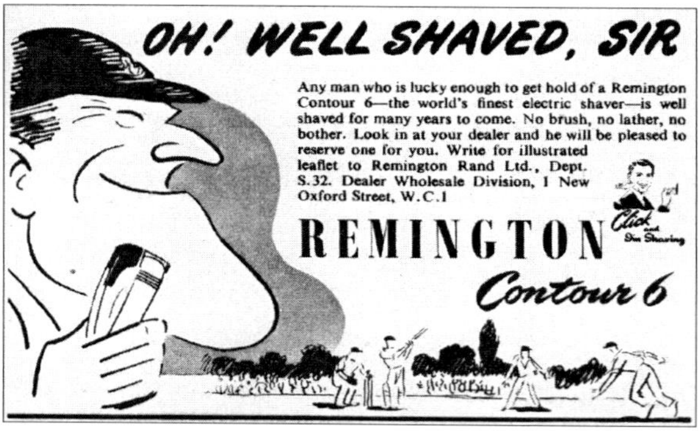

No. 3 Maison Beryl Hairdressers

In 1952 Maison Beryl looked after the ladies. Miss Beryl Watkins employed the latest technology, a perm machine comprising rods on wires which plugged into the electricity supply via an overhead socket. 'You have to suffer to be beautiful' must have comforted the ladies.

"I remember my mum going upstairs and having a sort of electric perm they did then, it frightened me! I thought 'What are they doing to mum?' and I ended up crying!" (AB12)

~ Turning left, the Street Trail continues up Market Street ~

No. 4 The Police Superintendent's House

There were no shops here in 1952. It was a private house and earlier in the century was where the Police Superintendent lived, keeping a watchful eye on the occupants of the police cells behind.

→ Look for . . . the scrolled stone signs on the front of the building ←

Nos. 5 to 8 Pippet Buildings, Market Street

Beyond the car park entrance is Pippet Buildings, numbers 5 to 8 Market Street. In 1952 it was pretty run down, by the 1960s derelict and by the 70s, facing demolition. The Bradford on Avon Preservation Trust, with the support of the local townspeople, fought heroically to protect the buildings, eventually organising their restoration in 1982, a project which subsequently gained a Civic Trust Award.

Its history began in the early 19th century when the land was bought in 1815 by a Bradford on Avon clothier, John Saunders. He appears to have had these buildings constructed on the site, quite possibly as purpose-built shops.

An enterprising man, Mr Saunders evidently saw his new project as a quality development and took pains to keep out the riff-raff. In 1817 his indenture stipulated that none of the shops could be used as a slaughterhouse or by a

> *"soapboiler, melter of tallow, printer, coppersmith, tanner, stonecutter, victualler... or any other dangerous, hazardous noisy noisome unwholesome or offensive trade or calling".*[59]

John Saunders' vision was rewarded. He might have been gratified to know that starting with William Bullock, a watchmaker who bought the end tenement at the top (now number 8) for £300, there have always been watchmakers and jewellers in Pippet Buildings. Starting with William Bullock in 1817, the tradition included Mr Titley at number 5 in 1948 and is carried on today by Ortons at numbers 6 and 7, so ensuring that every building in this terrace has been used by jewellers and watchmakers at some stage in its history.

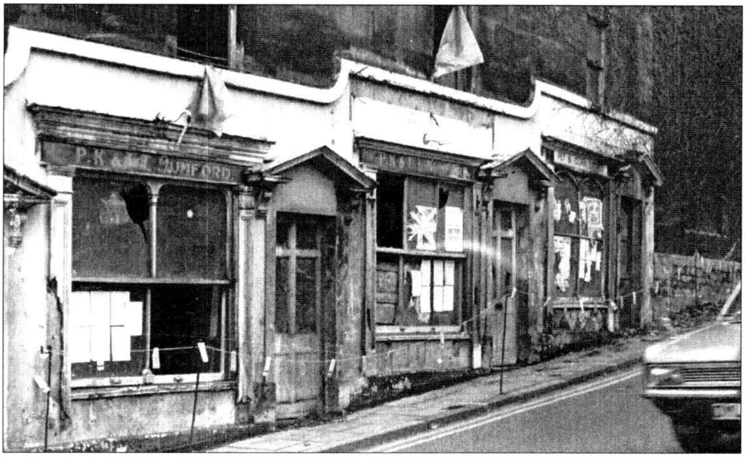

Pippet Buildings in the 1970s. Mumford's Greengrocers shop opened here in 1952.

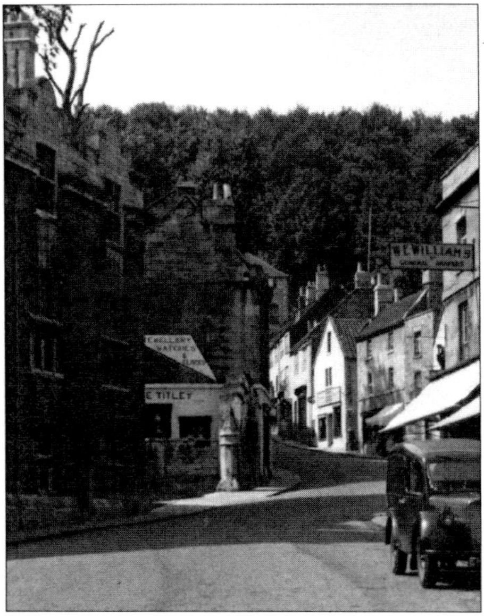

No. 5 J Titley, Watchmaker

In 1952 Mr J Titley ran his watch and clock making business here, having set up shop in 1948 when he bought the premises for £200. He was remembered by one local person as 'the man who put extra pieces into wedding rings for fingers swollen by work over the years.' Before that it was occupied by a tailor, and in the mid-19th century, delightful to imagine now, had housed a small school.

Nos. 6 & 7 P K Mumford, Fishmonger, Fruiterer

In 1952 this shop at numbers 6 and 7 changed hands from George Brown's Greengrocers to P K Mumford Greengrocers.

George Brown started out at number 5 in 1901 and by 1908 had taken over number 6 next door; the shop has remained combined ever since. After he died in 1950 the two shops were finally sold in 1952 to P K Mumford for £350 and Mr Mumford continued selling fruit, vegetables and wet fish.

> *"The greengrocery was on one side and fish on the other. I can remember going over there with my mother, with our ration books."* (AB12)

George Brown was also a wholesaler, with a warehouse in Bridge Street. When bananas started arriving again in the UK after the war, they were hung from the beams to ripen with heat from a small gas fire. Produce arrived from Covent Garden and Bristol to supply the local greengrocers.

> *"They had one big van. They went down Bristol early in the morning to the market, or . . . greengroceries would arrive by train and the coal yard was down by the railway station as well so that all came up in trucks."* (CB12)

Earlier there had been a shoemaker, barber and butcher going back to 1817 in number 7, and in number 6, a milliner, dressmaker, and a shoemaker.

No. 8 Pitts Corn Stores

In 1952 the shop at the top of the row held a small stock of pets and a large stock of pet food, mostly grain.

> *"My sister and myself, we bought guinea pigs, one each, but we didn't have them very long – he had them back!"* (AB12)

Before Pitts it was Stevens Grocers, run by 'the rather small and rotund Jack Stevens':

> *"He sold two sorts of cooked meat, one lot for pets and a very popular form called brawn for human beings. The back of the shop was in a very dilapidated state."*
>
> *"You could take a basin down and get home-made faggots and peas and he used to go out on a bicycle with a basket on front delivering cold meats and that to different people here. They were a nice couple. And she must have worked hard to keep all that up together because it was such a small shop and it must have all been done behind in whatever area they had at the back."* (JB12)

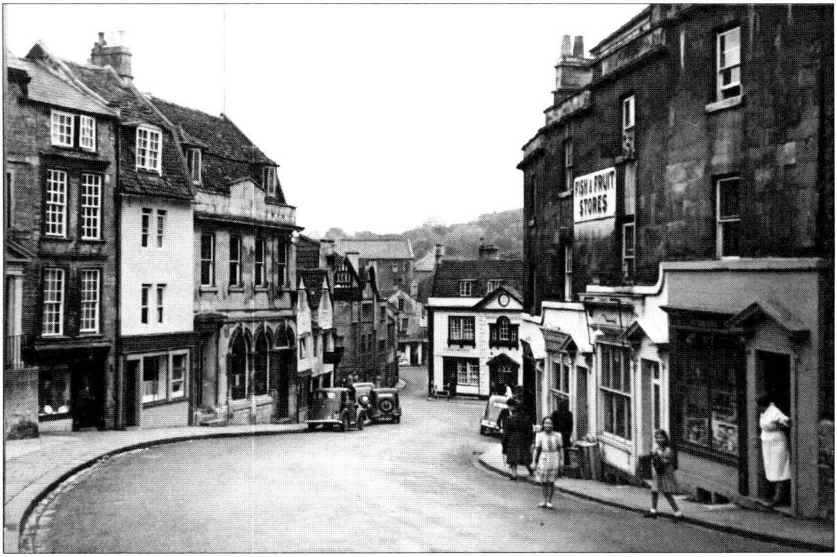

Faggots originated in the West Country and most recipes include pig's brains, although you could opt for sheep's brains for variety, with an appetising foamy broth to accompany the dish. They were sometimes known as Savoury Ducks, an early bit of spin which dates back to the Middle Ages.

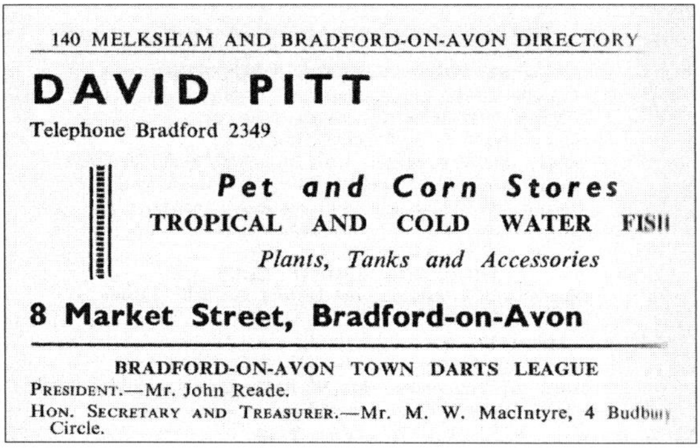

140 MELKSHAM AND BRADFORD-ON-AVON DIRECTORY

DAVID PITT

Telephone Bradford 2349

Pet and Corn Stores

TROPICAL AND COLD WATER FISH

Plants, Tanks and Accessories

8 Market Street, Bradford-on-Avon

BRADFORD-ON-AVON TOWN DARTS LEAGUE

President.—Mr. John Reade.

Hon. Secretary and Treasurer.—Mr. M. W. MacIntyre, 4 Budbury Circle.

In the previous century it was occupied by at least two generations of the same family of watchmakers, with the earliest record showing William Bullock in business in 1817. His son Arthur carried on the business here in 1861 and was still in business in 1891, with his wife Eleanor who made straw bonnets, and their eight children. Straw bonnet makers were down the pecking order from milliners, who dressed the basic bonnet shape with ribbons and flowers and made more intricate lace and muslin caps.[60]

It was occupied by Francis Everett, linen and woollen draper, in 1893, but had become a seed merchants by 1899.

~ The Street Trail continues over the road ~

In the 1950s numbers 10 to 14 Market Street were private houses although they had an earlier history of shopkeeping. In 1886 Joseph Bendle, Tea Dealer and Umbrella Maker, was busy juggling his two trades somewhere along this row. In 1911 number 13 housed a bakery and number 12, a watchmaker and jeweller. In the 1980s number 14 was a dress agency, run by former stuntwoman Bertie Golightly, so renowned that it eventually moved to London's Knightsbridge. She still has a shop in Marlborough, Wiltshire.

No. 15 F H Way, Radio, TV and Electrical Engineer

In 1952 this shop at number 15 had a small stock of televisions, probably unaware that these new-fangled devices would take off the following year as people rushed to buy them for the Queen's coronation.

"They supplied our first television here. We couldn't get very good reception; we had to have scaffold poles up in the air. We got it for the Coronation and everyone

came to watch our telly at our house in Church Street. It was a bit boring so the kids played outside, didn't they! I think we had an old KB television, that was a make in those days. Very small, black and white. Like a cabinet, square on the ground, upright with a top on, with bakelite knobs. You didn't get much television, only after about 6 o'clock at night for a couple of hours and that was it really!" (CB12)

This sounds like a superior model. Also available was the 14-inch table model with 'extra valves for relentless interference suppression and commanding cabinet-work in high-gloss, two-tone walnut' at the exorbitant price of 73 guineas. A high price to pay for such limited viewing: one hour in the afternoon, one hour at teatime and three hours in the evening. A second commercialised TV channel started in 1955.

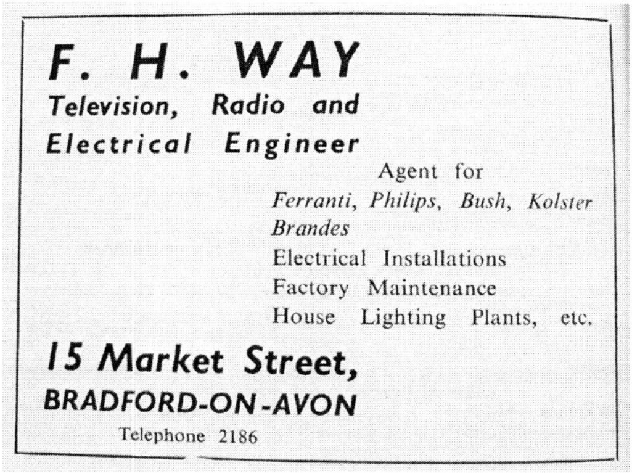

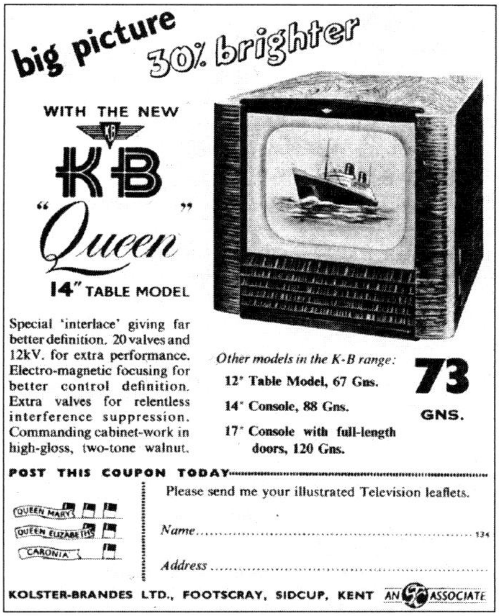

No. 16 Stan Green, Cycle Agent and Engineer

Back in 1952 cycling to work was commonplace and Stan Green had a thriving business.

> *"He did mopeds or small motorbikes as well and they had a petrol pump outside. I took my bike to be repaired there. He did it while you waited. In those days you could cycle up to Westbury Hill, we used to do that when we were eight or ten. Four or five of us, you just got on your bikes and cycled over there and no-one would worry. You didn't get any traffic to worry about. You just took your sandwiches and that was it."* (CB12)

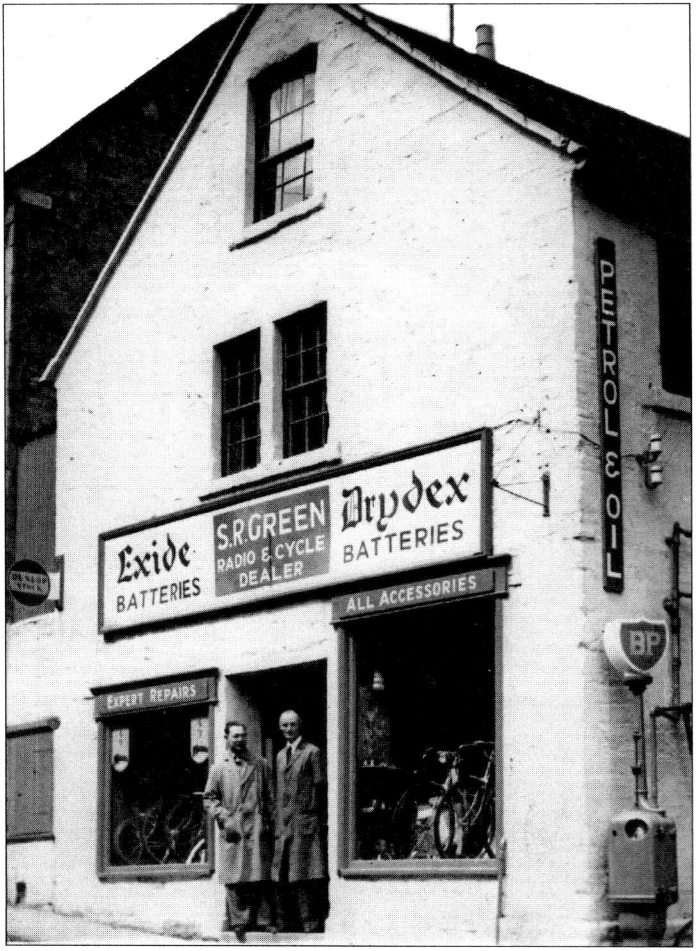

"He charged radio batteries. That was still in the days of the accumulator – rechargeable lead acid batteries. He had these glass accumulators with a handle over the top and you marched up there to get them charged. It was a completely and utterly ridiculous system because it was eventually replaced by battery eliminators which replaced the battery. Then the all-AC sets came in." (RS12)

In 1830 to 1871 George Summers the blacksmith was up the little alley alongside the shop.

By 1890 to 1922 Frank Summers was running the forge. Hard to imagine horses tethered here now, waiting to be shod.

→ Look for . . . the square concrete block on the corner of the alley which is where the BP petrol pump was fixed ←

No. 17 A Davis & Son, Fruiterers, Fishmongers

In 1952 17 Market Street was occupied by another of Bradford on Avon's many greengrocers and fishmongers. The shop was part of the Davis empire, the well-known local family which also had a greengrocers in the Shambles at this time. The Market Street shop, established in 1907, was run by Mrs Blake.

"We always went down to Mrs Blake's to get the fish. She had a misted glass in one side of her eye. She was very, very forthright. If you didn't ask the right thing, you got it, sort of style!" (JB12)

Greengrocers carried a far smaller selection of produce than today. Many people grew their own, we didn't import exotic fruit and veg from the other side of the globe – and shops stocked what was in season.

18 Market Street

In 1952 number 18 was a private house. In the 1960s it was opened up as a DIY shop by Ken Applegates.

No. 19 Perrett's Basket Shop

In 1952 these hairdresser's premises were listed in the *West Wiltshire Trade Directory* as A G Perrett, Boot and Shoe Repairer but it was more commonly known as the "basket shop".

"He used to go off with his little cart which he pushed along. How did he manage? With difficulty! But there wasn't any traffic about much. He didn't have a stick but

everyone knew he was blind." (CB12)

"He did do some amazing baskets, there was no two ways about it, he used to hang them all outside. As an eleven year old boy as I was then everybody called it the basket shop." (JB12)

No. 27 Antiques and Curios

In 1952 this was a small antiques shop, now an estate agent. The business was run by H J Pitt, part of the same family which at that time ran the Pet Shop and Corn Stores over the road at number 8.

Vibeka Jenkins, who with her husband Andrew bought these premises together with numbers 25 and 26 in 1963, told me that when they renovated the top floor of this little shop she was astonished to find many thousands of rusty dressmaking pins heaped under the floorboards, no doubt dating back to its use as a milliner's workshop. From 1887 to 1893 it was occupied by George Willcox, watch and clockmaker and by 1899 Edgar Payne was in place, moving to the Shambles by 1903.

No. 28 Mrs Ann's Fish Shop

In 1952 Mrs Edith Ann did a roaring trade in fish and chips.

"The counter was high on one end and lower on the other and because we were only children we went round that end so we could see over the top. And they had the fat cookers along the side, and they would turn round and put it in the white paper and wrap it in newspaper, it was always in newspaper. You could get a pennyworth of chips then and the fish was only sixpence or thereabouts, it was very cheap but it was very popular. You would queue, they were very busy, very busy always. But the adults went along the front and the children who came in on their own went along the side and they got served separately with a pennyworth of chips and you used to get that wrapped up in paper and they used to put the vinegar and salt on it. They ask you now but they used to just put it on then. They were lovely fish and chips." (JS12)

In 1953 Mrs Ann is also listed as an agent of Modeluxe Drycleaners, not an obvious combination one would have thought.

"I didn't know that Mrs Ann was a branch of Modeluxe Cleaners. She may have well been but all the clothes would have stunk of fish and chips, wouldn't they? It's obvious, it's bizarre to me, that!" (JB12)

In 1887 Bradford's Post Office was set up in these premises, run by Charles Rawling who had a printing works in the Town Club building next door. By 1925 it was W & O Manners Fish Bar. This was the golden era of fish and chips, when many industrial towns would have had a shop on almost every street, totalling about 35,000 outlets in the UK.[61]

→ Look for . . . the tiled floor inside dates back to its time as a fish and chip shop ←

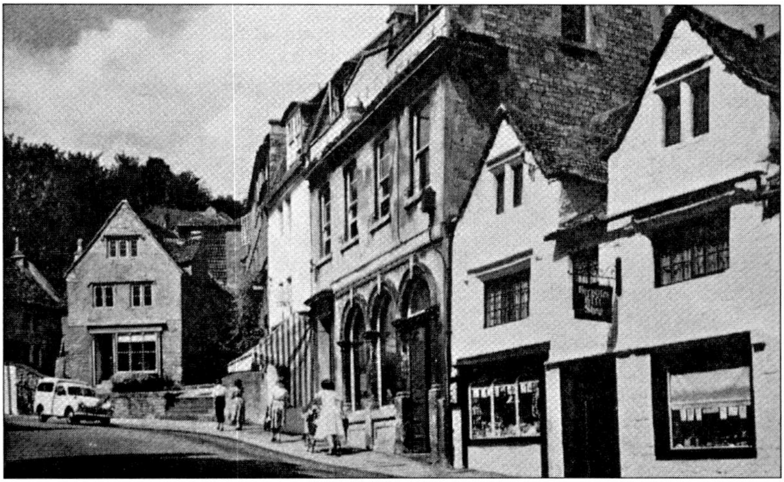

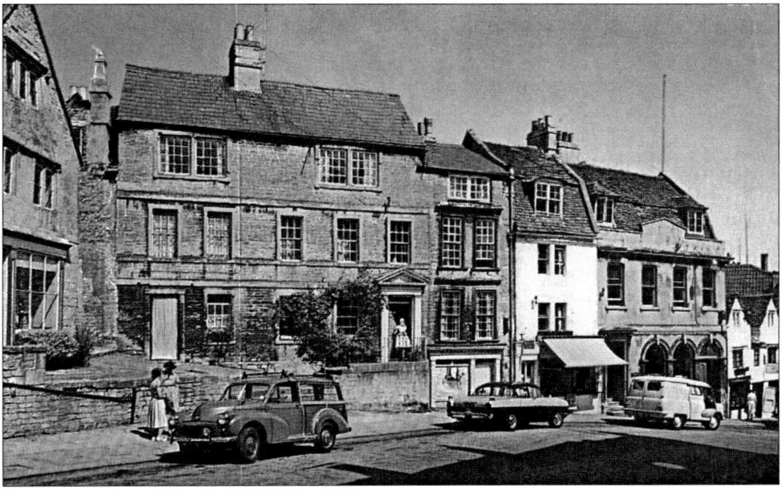

Market Street, around 1961

No. 31 Grey Tiles Gift Shop

In 1952 this lovely twin-gabled shop sold china ornaments, greetings cards and presents.

> *"Miss Ross used to own Grey Tiles, proper little spinster lady, very smart, posh you know."* (CB12)

In 1869 Miss L L England the Milliner was advertising 'straw bonnets, caps, velvets, feathers, French flowers, etc.' In 1895 it was occupied by Miss Rose Andrew, dressmaker. By 1911 it was The Bradford Toilet Saloon and Tobacco Stores. A marvellous ad in Dotesio's Year Book and Directory announces: 'For First Class Haircutting, Singing, Shampooing and Shaying. Strict Attention, Cleanliness and Civility Assured.' Could this have been Bradford's very own Barbershop Quartet? Or did they just miss out the 'e'?

→ Look for . . . the horizontally sliding sash windows on the first floor dating back to the mid to late 17th century, 'possibly the last surviving in Bradford', in one of the town's oldest buildings.[62] **←**

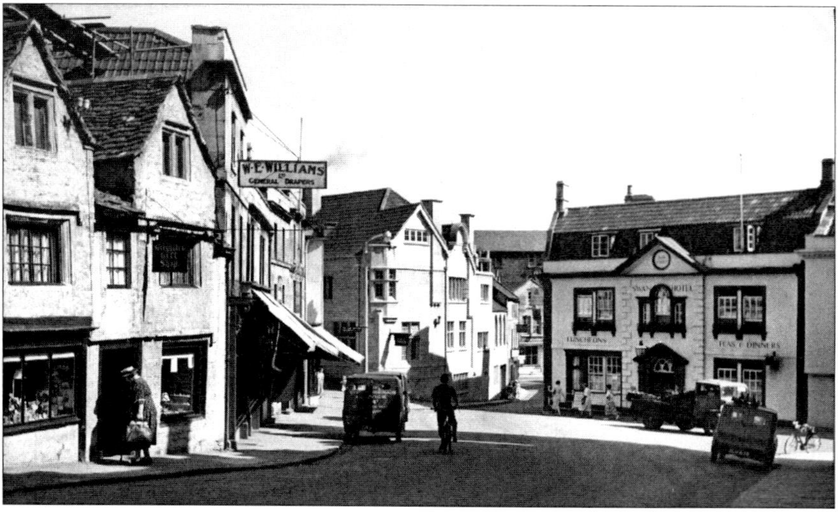

No. 32 W E Williams, Ladies Outfitters, Drapers

In 1952 there was a busy drapers in the smart premises now occupied by an antiques business. They would have been in competition with Goodalls in Silver Street and the Co-op drapers in the Shambles.

> *"If you couldn't get it at Goodalls you went to Williams . . . or vice versa! But I don't remember trying things on. They didn't have changing rooms - not in Bradford!"* (JS12)

> *"I can remember when stockings came in boxes, folded inside. It was lovely, all laid out, and the vests and petticoats were folded in slide out drawers. Stockings were four shillings and eleven pence (29p). Compared with wages stockings were quite expensive."* (AB12)

> *"I remember I had a sixpence (2½p) which was a lot of money in those days and I dropped it down the grating in front of the shop and I went in to the shop, but of course they couldn't do anything about it and I couldn't understand why they couldn't get my sixpence back! My sixpence might still be down there!"* (AB12)

New materials such as nylon, developed before the Second World War but then restricted, were hugely in demand after 1945. Interestingly, when the seamless nylon stocking was introduced in 1952, ladies would not be tempted away from the seamed variety, which gave a clear signal it was a stocking and not a humble bare leg. This wonder fabric had its problems, though. Housewives were frustrated to find that their nylon petticoats, available for eight shillings and eleven pence (44p), quickly yellowed, particularly if dried in direct sunlight, and the static build up caused sparks to fly. Tights were not introduced until 1959.

The shop has had a connection with clothes for much of its history. In 1887 it was Southwell's Boot and Shoe Shop and in 1911 was the London Drapery Co, run by a Mrs Pearce. In 1867 it was occupied by Joseph Bendle, umbrella maker, having moved here from further up the road and his son continued after him in 1895.

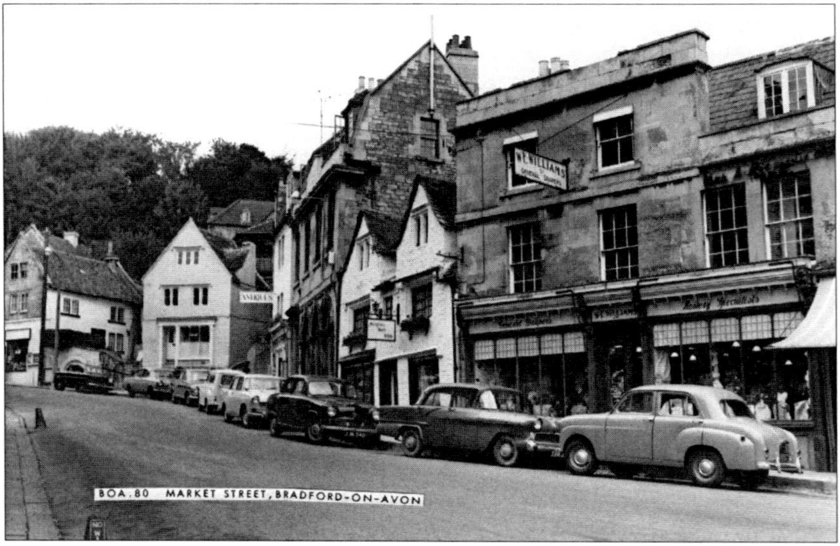
BOA.80 MARKET STREET, BRADFORD-ON-AVON

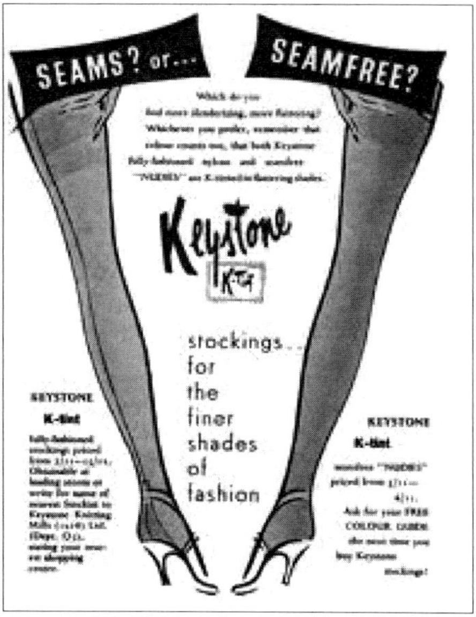
SEAMS? or...
SEAMFREE?
Keystone
stockings... for the finer shades of fashion
KEYSTONE
K-tint
KEYSTONE
K-tint

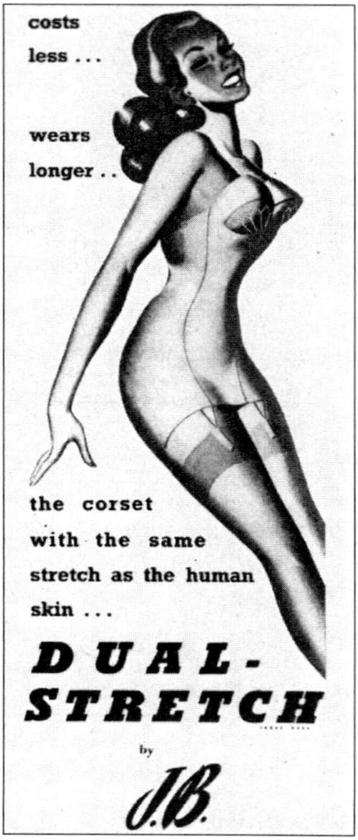
costs less ...
wears longer ..
the corset with the same stretch as the human skin ...
DUAL-STRETCH
by
J.B.

No. 33 Uncles & Sons, Boot and Shoe Shop

In 1952 this was a popular shoe shop, now a gift shop. Mr Mervyn Uncles was a local magistrate and commanded much respect in the town. The Uncles shoe shop empire was started by his grandfather, Mark Uncles, at the bottom of Market Street in 1888. His son Rowland moved here in 1934 and it continued trading as a shoe shop until 1987. Mr Uncles had a second shoe shop, Dodges, at 37 Silver Street, and the family had outlets in Pickwick, Corsham and Bath.

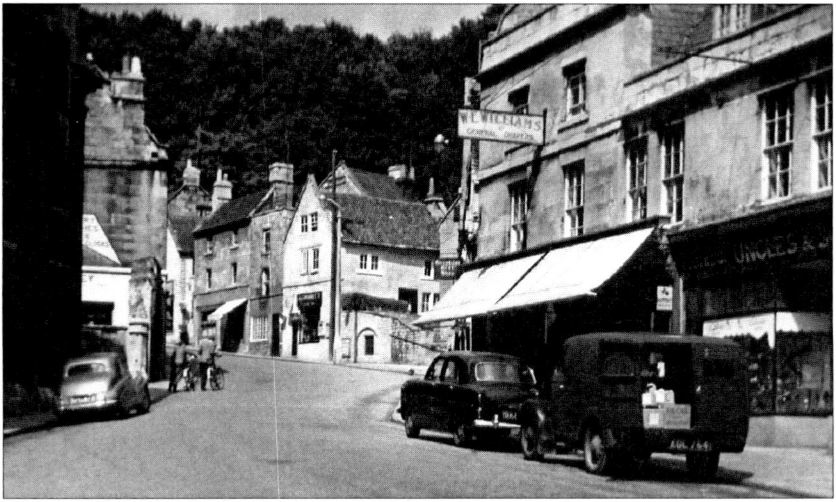

Uncles advertised four width fittings for children.

"In those days you had those awful x-ray things that you put your feet in. You'd put your shoe on, put your foot in, stand up and they'd take an x-ray of your feet to show where your toes were. You could sit there for five minutes and do this that and the other and get your feet really fried - it was ridiculous. I don't think an awful lot was known then about x-rays. It was pretty dire. And they make a fuss now about luminous paint on watches!" (WS and RS12)

"He had one of those long spindles and a last to hammer the soles on. And they had these old Singer 29Ks which were hand-operated with a very long narrow foot to get inside the shoe so you could stitch. It was all out the back where you couldn't see it because it was more upmarket than a cobblers."(RS12)

"You always had to go upstairs and it used to take a long time to get a pair of shoes. No-one hurried in those days, did they?" (CB12)

Earlier businesses on this site include John Mundy, Ironmonger, in 1848, Miss Alexander's milliners in 1887 and in 1899 Thomas Mobbs was combining three trades. He ran an ironmongers, and doubtless having discovered how useful they could be for his second job as agent for a Parcel Carrier, was also selling bicycles. By 1911 the shop was an ironmongers known as 'Ye Padlocke'.

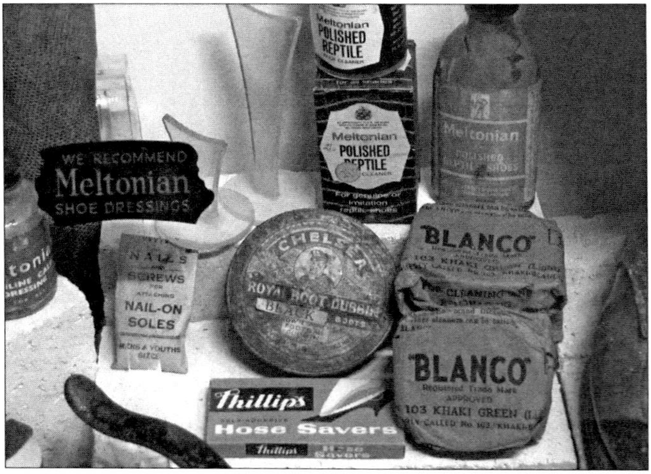

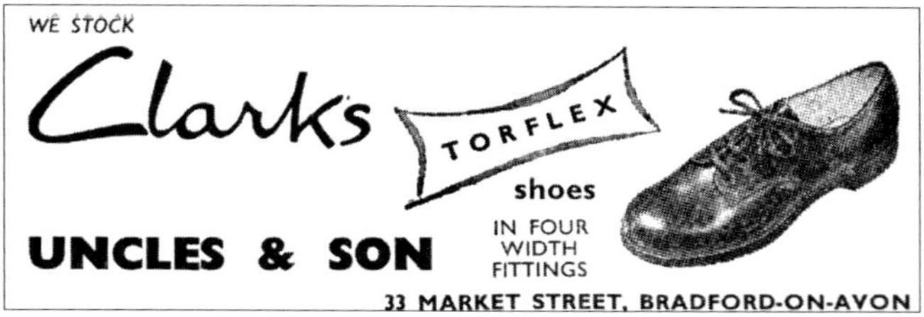

Items from Uncles can be seen in the Bradford on Avon Museum

→ Look for . . . the Uncles sign on a small cast iron stop valve cover on the pavement in front of the shop. Berkeley Uncles and Son had a foundry in Trowbridge Road and were related to the shoe shop Uncles ←

No. 34 Fanny Pinchin's Sweet Shop

In 1952 this very appealing little shop was a confectioners, run by the redoubtable Fanny Pinchin. Miss Pinchin weighed up sweets for several decades and by the 1950s one suspects she might have lost her early enthusiasm for shopkeeping. It was said to be very old fashioned. One customer recalls it smelt strongly of cat pee and another remembers that in the 1930s:

> *"If you looked through the window at night you could see the mice running all over the sweets."* (JL97)[63]

Unusually for a sweet shop, children seemed to have to screw up their courage to enter. One small boy had his sweet coupons refused and another remembers her mother calling by one day to buy peppermints.

> *"Fanny said, 'Can't you see we're closed!' And she wouldn't get up out of the chair; 'What do you want?' sort of thing. She lived at the back of the shop and there was a little glass window with lacy curtains so she could see you come in…and the quicker she could get us out the better!" (JS12)*

Sweets were sold by the quarter (125g) which would have cost about fourpence. Children would have asked for a pennyworth – and probably got short shrift from Fanny when they did.

The shop dates from the 1700s. In 1875 this was Martha Grist's Berlin Wool Depot. Berlin woolwork, more commonly known as needlepoint, was a phenomenally popular pastime in England with around 14,000 patterns available in 1840. In 1881 the shop had become a confectionery and fancy goods shop, run by cousins Anna Bedford and Mary Horton and in 1903 George Sims turned it into a 'Fancy Repository', then Kendalls Tailors in 1910 to 1914.

No. 35 Nichols & Bushell, Family Grocers

In the 1950s this restaurant was Nichols & Bushell, regarded as the best of the town's grocers. A resident of the town remembers:

> *"It was wonderful! A real old-fashioned shop. Wooden floors and the smells were wonderful - bacon and ground coffee. No self-service, it was all behind the counter as you went in. On the left it was all dry things like biscuits and flours and on the other side it was bacon and butter.*
>
> *Nothing was pre-packed then. It was all in big sacks and the sugar was put into pound packs with blue paper. Butter was cut off and patted into shape with wooden boards."* (WS12)

> *"They used to deliver. You'd give them a list and they'd drop it off to you, or you'd go back and get it later."* [The delivery van can be seen in the photograph on page 74] (CB12)

As was common in shops in those days, money and food were kept apart.

"There was a cashier at the back of the shop. They made out a chit and this was what you took to pay the woman. She took your money and this was elementary hygiene to keep handling of money separate to the goods, which was a step in the right direction!" (RS12)

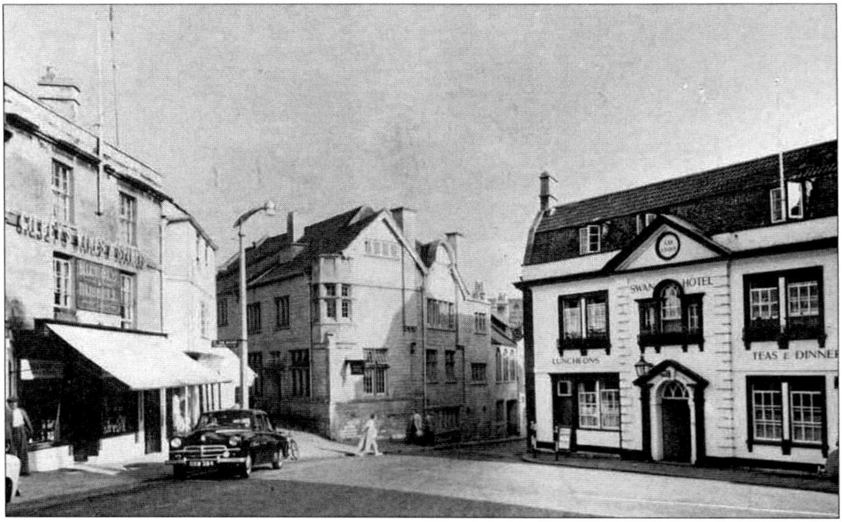

All the shops along this west facing side of Market Street had wide cloth canopies suspended out into the street, protecting the goods in the windows from strong sunlight.

The shop was occupied by Thomas Smart, grocer, corn factor and tallow chandler early in the nineteenth century, then John Silby's Boot and Shoe Business from 1854 to 1890. Albert Nichols is first registered here in 1891 as a Patent Medicine Vendor and Wine and Spirit Merchant and by 1911 the shop was a grocers. It became Nichols & Bushell soon after 1915 and they stayed in business until the 1960s.

No. 36 Madame Soul

In the 1950s number 36, now a building society, was a drapers and milliners run by the Belgian lady Madame Marie Soul who first set up the business in 1904. With a foreign accent and a whiff of sophistication, she was regarded as an exotic foreigner by the children of Bradford on Avon.

Clothes rationing ended in 1949 and people were enjoying the chance to buy new for a change.

"I can remember mother going in one day and wanting a hat. My mother had a

bottle green outfit and she was going to a silver wedding so Madame Soul came out with a lime green hat and mother wasn't very impressed with the lime hat to go with bottle green but Madame Soul insisted 'Green goes very well with green!' She had this sort of broken accent and I think mother went to Bath in the end to find her hat!" (JS12)

In those days men and women invariably wore hats, with a price of around ten shillings (50p). Dress was still conventional with teenagers appearing to make the transition from child to young adult overnight, dressing just like their parents. It wasn't until the end of the 1950s that this stuffy, formal approach was thrown over, hats were abandoned and a fresh young fashion emerged.

This shop had a long tradition of trading as a draper and outfitter from at least 1881, when Mary Ann Livings occupied it as The Drapery Bazaar. In 1903 it was owned by the Misses C & D Boorman and it continued as an outfitter right through to the 1960s.

→ Look for . . . the ornate window mullions with nicely appropriate draping detail ←

The photograph below shows a schoolboy in shorts and cap looking in at the window of Fanny Pinchin's sweet shop. He has a rolled up towel under his arm and might well be on his way to the old swimming baths, situated where the Library and Museum are now.

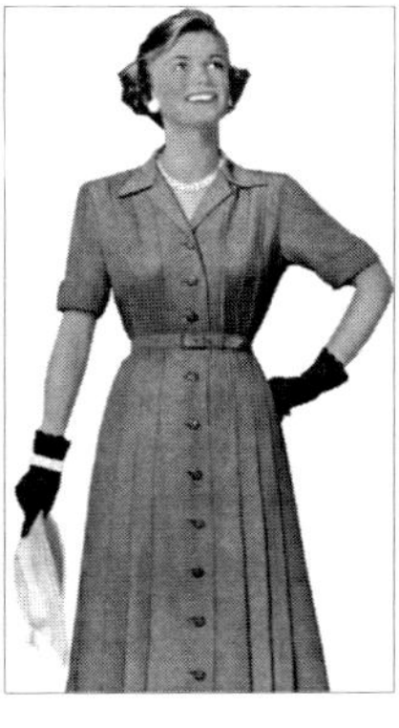

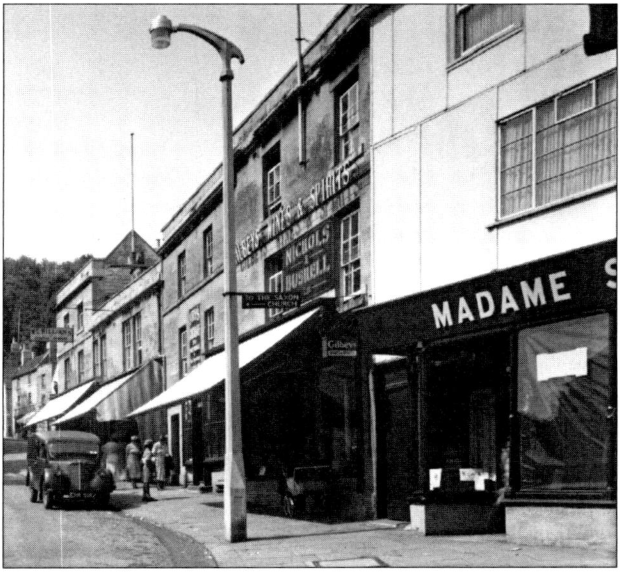

Mums felt secure leaving babies outside shops while they popped inside. The pram outside Nichols & Bushell has a large basket suspended at the back, handy for the daily shopping trip. Grocers' window displays rarely deviated from the tried and tested pyramid of dusty canned goods.

Madame Soul's window displays another typical 1950s feature: a tinted plastic sheet, usually yellow, to prevent the goods from fading in direct sunlight.

~ Market Street continues down past the end of the Shambles ~

Rear Access to the old Post Office

In 1952 this was the entrance to the old Post Office basement where the vans would pull in off the street and load up. To save them the struggle of backing out once they were loaded, a turntable was installed which turned the vans around, ready to drive out nose first. The turntable still survives inside the building.

Jack Stafford remembers painting the top windows of the Post Office.

> *"To get to the top gables we had two long ladders tied together and to get the right angle the ladder was about two feet out into the roadway with a man standing on the bottom rung. Only one car at a time could get past. But then there was nothing much coming past anyway. That little shop in the side wall of The Swan was quite a busy butchers at the time. You wouldn't have called it the wrong side of the road in those days. No traffic problem at all."* (JS97)[64]

Over the road you can see an old shop, now empty and definitely past its best. The building is late 17th century. It was known to be a butcher in 1848, and then Carter's Butchers in the late 19th century. In 1906 Albert Mayell had a china and greengrocery business here, displaying his goods out on the street, unthinkable today. In the 1930s it had reverted once again to a butchers, run by Bert Scrine who went on to open The Three Gables cafe with his new wife, Edie Baxter, who worked in the Co-op cake shop.[65] More recently it was a restroom for the staff of the Swan Hotel.

→ Look for . . . the beautiful painted sign on the wall of the hotel "Swan Hotel, Family & Commercial" ←

No. 37 Mrs Coles' Fancy Stores

This small shop, now an estate agent, was popularly known in the 1950s as Mrs Coles' Penny Pop Shop. One resident remembers calling in to buy "penny pops" on his way back from the swimming baths. Although food hygiene testing was in place it evidently wasn't rigorously enforced, as a local resident recalls:

> *"Mr and Mrs Coles sold penny ice lollies. At that time my father was on the Council and he used to sometimes come back and say, don't go and buy any ice cream or ice lollies there - they haven't quite passed the test! The Public Health Officer for the local Urban Council would visit and take a sample away."* (CB)

RS and WS remember:

> *"Rationing was in in the Fifties so you didn't have many sweets. You made your own sweets. One's mother concocted all sorts of strange things and called them sweets. But sometimes we used to go down [to Mrs Coles] in our lunchtime, against school rules, from Fitzmaurice School and buy coconut ice – bright pink and white."*

Mrs Coles would have been selling the new sweets of the day. Polo mints were introduced in 1948 and Bounty in 1951.

In the early 20th century there was a lovely stone canopy over the door which opened directly onto this narrow street.

→ Look for . . . the outline of the low doorway on the side wall, now filled in by limestone blocks ←

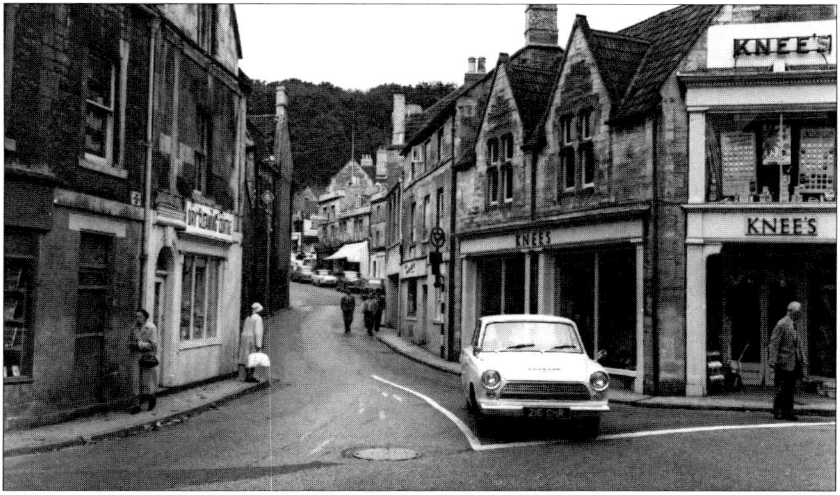

No. 38 Knees Corner

In 1952 Knees homeware store occupied the open space now occupied by the Fat Fowl's tables and chairs, which led to this part of town being known as Knee's Corner.

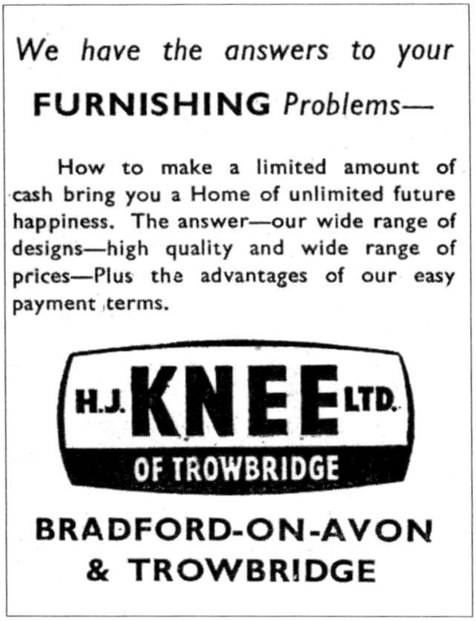

Knees opened here in 1905 and the store was eventually pulled down in 1967 to 'improve' traffic movement.

There was a desperate shortage of housing in 1950s Britain. Many people rented rooms but after the deprivations of wartime home improvement was sweeping the nation. Times were hard and a bit of lino and a rag rug were often the only affordable makeover, with carpets and three-piece suites invariably bought on tick. Knees was well aware of the struggle and optimistically advised in the 1952 town directory, "How to make a limited amount of cash bring you a Home of unlimited future happiness."

> *"They had all this utility furniture there, with a Utility sign on the back, but I think mainly we just bought household stuff, curtain rail, curtain hooks and things like that. You just tagged along with your mother and her boring trip!"* (WS12)

Knees had a huge range of stock:

> *"It seemed a bit higgledy piggledy, with big glass windows, two doorways one at an angle at the front and one at the side."* (CB12)

One of the best selling ranges of crockery in the 1950s was Homemaker, a jazzy black and white design only available from Woolworths. A full set cost thirty one shillings (£1.55), cups and saucers were one shilling and threepence (6½ p) and teapots ten shillings (50p). A teapot recently sold on Ebay for £900!

The building was the White Hart Inn two hundred years ago but the British and Foreign Temperance Society succeeded in shutting down drinking within its walls. in 1845 it became a coffee house and then, the final twist, a Temperance Hotel. It was acquired and renovated by Knees in 1905. Knees still has branches in Trowbridge and Malmesbury and is the oldest family owned department store in the West Country, dating back to 1879.

~ The Street Trail continues past the Fat Fowl and up Silver Street, before turning into the Shambles ~

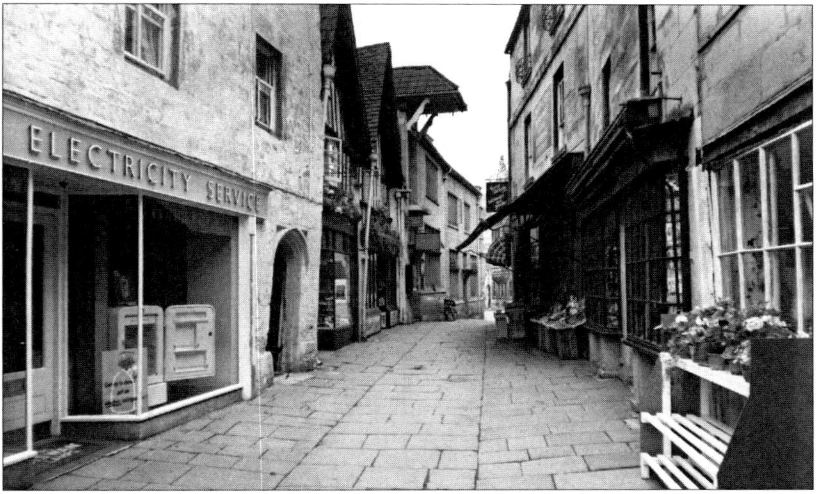

The Shambles

People have shopped in the immediate area of The Shambles for around a thousand years. The name derives from *scammel*, an Anglo-Saxon word meaning stool or bench where goods were displayed, mainly meat, and so the word also came to mean slaughterhouse. Here in Bradford it might well have derived from the medieval butchers' stalls in the old Market Hall at the east end of the street. Parts of Tillions, in the stone buildings on the south-east corner of the Shambles are 14th century and the two wood-framed buildings further along date from the 16th century.

The Market Hall butted up against Tillions. It survived from medieval times until it was demolished in the 1820s when it became unsafe. The ground floor entrance faced the lower side of Silver Street and was used as a crockery store in the late 18th century. The floor above housed butcher's stalls within an open colonnade facing up Coppice Hill. Wooden partitions were in place between the plain stone columns and the central column doubled as the whipping post for the local bad lads.

A staircase led to the room above where court sessions took place. The top storey with its projecting diamond-paned windows collapsed in 1800 but the butchers continued trading for another 25 years, with continued calls for repairs falling on deaf ears. One night the rest of the fragile structure collapsed. Rumour spread that it had been helped along its way and one lucky chap carted off the remains for the bargain sum of 20 shillings. It's probable that the materials are now incorporated in other local buildings.[66]

This would have been the focal point of the town and the scene of barbaric entertainments such as 'flinging at cocks', a sport recorded as taking place here in 1731.[67] As with bull-baiting, the practice of throwing weighted sticks at tethered cockerels had all but died out by the early 19th century, shamefully due more to complaints of public nuisance rather than animal cruelty. This was also the site of the town pillory and, more chilling, the stake where Thomas Traynell was burnt to death for heresy in 1532. The market eventually moved to Market Street in 1841.

→ Look for . . . the roof line of the old Market Hall, seen high up on the side of the Shambles building ←

No. 6a Southern Electricity Board

In 1952 the SEB had their showrooms in these large premises at the end of the Shambles.

Housewives in the 1950s would pop in here to pay their bills and watch encouraging cookery demonstrations on the new appliances.

The photograph shows a 'fridge proudly displayed in the window alongside a sign, 'Get up to date – get an electric refrigerator!' In the 1950s, the typical home would have had a cooker, a vacuum cleaner costing around £14 – hugely expensive at that time - and a radio, but only 33% of homes had a washing machine. A small single tub and hand wringer cost around £30, about a month's wages for many people.

Only 15% of families had a 'fridge. The usual alternative was a 'meat safe', a small cupboard with a metal grille on the front to allow air to circulate. Freezers and tumble dryers were practically unheard of.

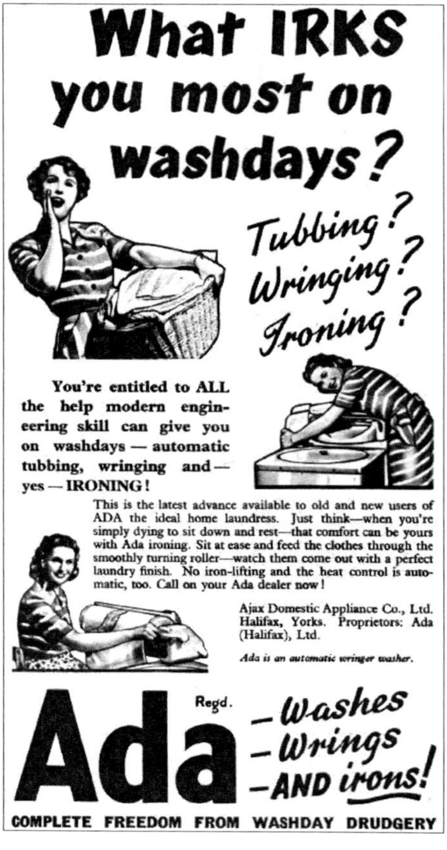

There was an electricity sub-station immediately below the shop:

"the most archaic piece of machinery in the western hemisphere" - and the further basement was used as a repair workshop. (JB11)

The building used to be a coffee shop run by Mrs Green, popular with the poor of the parish. She sold baked faggots for a penny, hot pea soup and rice pudding.[68] The basement was originally the town prison, extending right under the adjacent shops, and in use as early as 1790.

The building is on the site of the Royal Oak Inn, with a 15th century doorway still intact next to the shop. This is one of the oldest buildings in Bradford, with elements that date from the 14th century. Records of the pub go back to 1798 and it finally closed in 1912.

No. 7 Tudor Café

In 1952 Miss Nellie Slade ran a café and sweet shop from these old premises which date back to the 16th century.

"When we were very young we used to sit on the glass counter to choose our sweets." (CB12)

Miss Slade advertised 'dainty teas' but a resident remembers she also had a small library of books at the back of the shop and on occasions would serve take-away coffee in one of her own pots for the local shopkeepers to take back to their premises.

In the 1970s the new owner knocked through the adjoining wall connecting this shop to the newsagent next door, to create one larger shop. The wall was replaced in 2011.

This shop was occupied in 1841 by Robey, china and earthenware dealer.[69]

Later came Ellen Cabell, a confectioner, W Bailey's Hairdressers and in 1895, Miss Emma Fishlock, Pork Butcher.

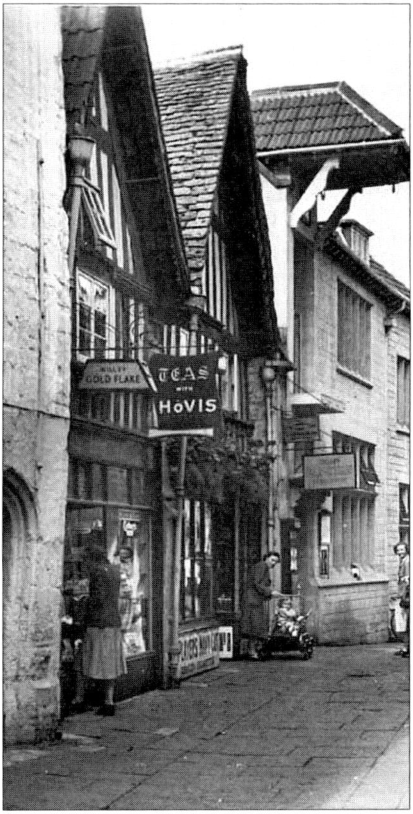

These two shops, together with Tillions at the end, are believed to be the only wood-framed buildings in Bradford.

No. 8 Higgs Tobacconist

In 1952 number 8 was Higgs Tobacconist:

> *"And very small it was too. Two people in there and it was full up. . . . they lived above it and their kitchen and dining room was at the back of the shop".* (JB11)

> *"They used to sell stationery and pens and notebooks but cigarettes and tobacco was the big seller. Most people smoked then."* (CB12)

In the 1950s, smoking had no negative associations. 'For your throat's sake, smoke Craven A' and 'More doctors smoke Camels than any other cigarette' were the reassuring adverts of the day.

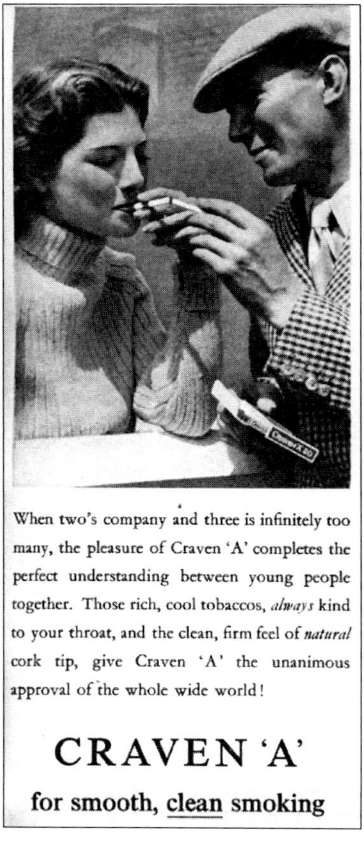

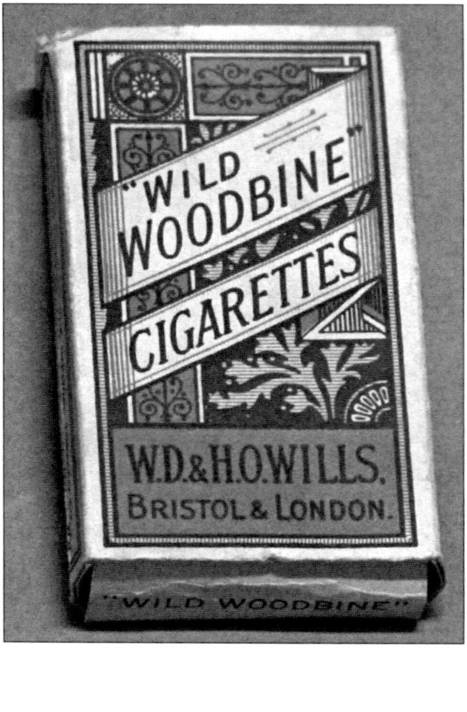

"They used to sell tobacco loose in big stoneware jars and they'd spoon it out and weigh it." (RS12)

There was a serious fire here in the 1930s which one resident remembers was hindered by something of a clash between the Bradford and the Trowbridge fire brigades and with the dramatic addition of a small baby being thrown to safety from a top window.

The building was saved, but the front elevation was badly damaged and replaced in about 1937. (JB11)

"It was impossible to get near the shop next day because of the thousands of wasps which were attracted by the sugary mass of melted sweets."[70]

In 1841 this was Dainton's greengrocers and in 1895 Henry Holly, greengrocer. By 1911 it was Fred Archard, tobacconist and hairdresser, before he moved to the top of Silver Sreet. It had an enamel sign outside announcing Shaving Saloon, along with the usual red and white striped pole.

No. 9 Post Office

In 1952 this was the Post Office in Bradford on Avon, occupying the whole building along to the corner, built in 1901. It was extended in 1936 when the old Co-op Grocers on this site was demolished.

Jack Gingell, born in Bradford in 1916, remembers working there:

"We were chased out of the Shambles with rats. They used to come out into the shop at night and we were open 'til 8 o'clock then. We packed up bags of sugar – we used to stop and do that for an hour at night to help us in the morning. The cellar came out under The Swan.

Well that cellar, that used to hold all our cheese that we sold in the shop above, you see. . . .fifty six pounds of cheese, two of those in a crate about three feet high, there was a hundredweight of cheese in there. Half of one of those blocks would have been eaten in any one night by those rats. That will give you an idea of how many rats were running through the Shambles, coming from the river. They used to come out in the shop and the women used to scream out the front door.

Right opposite our shop was Mr Davis, the fruiterer, and he used to sit up in his bedroom window with a small bore gun and the rats used to come out and go along the gutters along the outside of the building and he fired at them with his gun, Albert Davis." (JG10)

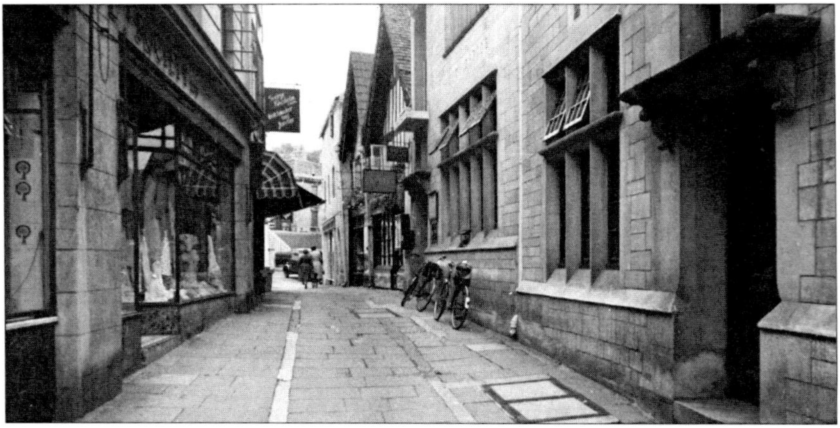

The Post Office was on a site previously occupied by a Georgian building which housed Taylor's Drapers for much of the 19th century, from at least 1822 to 1890. Somewhere on its premises it also accommodated in 1887 James England, razor strop maker and his wife, Eliza, greengrocer. She was still there in 1895 after he had died. In 1910 it was Arthur Wheeler's Outfitters and later the first Co-op Grocers before it moved down to Silver Street.

The old shop was demolished in 1930 to build this Post Office, as an extension to the Post Office next door. Very sadly, the Post Office closed on this site in 2013, after over a hundred years of service in the Shambles.

The building on the south-west corner of the Shambles and Market Street was part of the Post Office in 1952. It was built in 1901, replacing a ramshackle old building which had been occupied in 1841 by Dainton's greengrocers and William Clement, a young tailor, by William Bowden's fish shop in 1895 and, by 1900, William Earle's Ironmongery business. Canon Jones believed the Scribbling Horse Alehouse might have been squeezed somewhere in here.

→ Look for . . . the rare monogram of the uncrowned King Edward VIII displayed on the front wall of the building. This is one of only two Post Offices in the country to have a plaque dedicated to Edward, who abdicated before his coronation. The year 1935 is marked on the drainpipe hopper. ←

→ Look for the old postage stamp dispensers. Inside are the original beautiful tiled floor, cornices and wooden fittings ←

~ The shops continue on the north side the The Shambles with Ex Libris ~

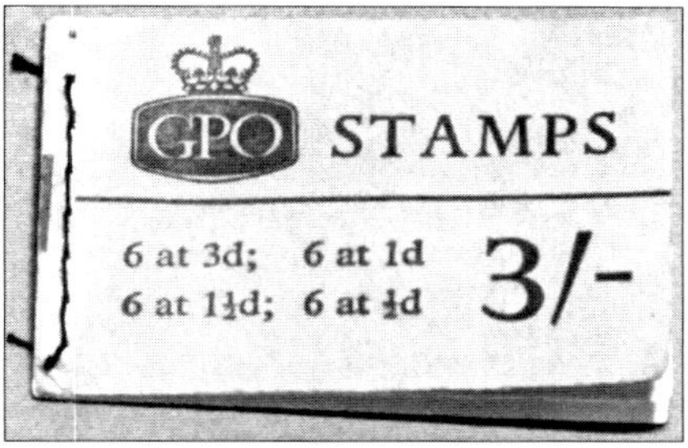

No. 1 The Co-operative Butchers

In the 1950s this bookshop was occupied by one of four butchers in the centre of town, all within 100 metres of each other.

As AB noted:

> *"There must have been a lot of people shopping in Bradford (in the 1950s) because we had a lot of shops that sold the same thing." (AB12)*

Butchers had sawdust on the floor and a separate cashier in a cubicle, usually a woman, so the butchers, invariably men, didn't have to handle the money – a benefit for both butcher and customer! Chicken was a Sunday dinner luxury, not an everyday staple. A local butcher in the Fifties remembered the meat acquiring a bit of a bloom. It didn't mean it was inedible, quite the reverse – it was considered better for being around and was quite safe for up to fourteen days.

> *"The Co-op butchers had the counter at the front and the meat hanging up and they used to go down the passageway to the back to get the meat out."* (CB12)

This building and the one next door at number 2 were built in 1930 to house the new butcher and drapers for the Bradford on Avon Co-operative Society, replacing earlier buildings. This work was carried out at the same time as the handsome Georgian building at 33 Silver Street was being brutally knocked about to accommodate the new Co-op grocers. They must have employed the same builders; the beautiful wall tiles which are still visible inside the bookshop here are exactly the same as those in the Co-op grocers, now hidden behind stud walling.

The Co-op butchers closed down in 1968.

→ Look for . . . the ornate wall tiles which date from the 1930s. In the photograph opposite you can see winning rosettes pinned up on these tiles in the window. The green marble fascia on this shop and the one next door was installed at the same time ←

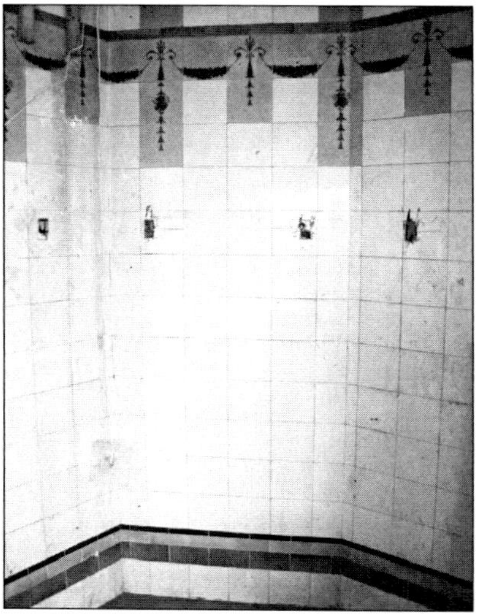

The 1920s' tiles in the old Silver Street Co-op grocers, identical to those in The Shambles' Co-op Butchers. Both sets of tiles are still there

No. 2 The Co-operative Drapers

In 1952 the Co-op Drapers occupied these large premises at number 2. The upper floor is largely unchanged since then, with the original fittings still in place. Like the butchers next door, it closed in 1968.

> *"There was a lovely service and I had several things made there. And you could buy all your sheets, blankets, curtains. You could choose all your materials. There's nothing like that in Bradford anymore." (DP11)*

> *"They used to have some pretty little pincushions in the window which used to attract me as a little girl. These little crinoline ladies, a little china top and then a crinoline where you could stick your pins in when you did your sewing."* (JS12)

> *"I went to work at the Co-operative and in our drapery shop we had this lovely phone on the wall and I think you wound it up and you had one single earpiece and you talked into the mouth piece. That was in the '60s, very old-fashioned!"* (AB12)

Dressmaking was common in most households but during the war when cloth material was in short supply, housewives took to altering and adjusting their clothes to create something new. Make do and mend was the watchword, even after the war had ended. But as fabric became more available, the trend for home-made clothes picked up again, and dress patterns sales rocketed, helped no doubt by the cost savings. Woolworths advised thrifty housewives that garments could be made for one tenth the cost of a new item.

There was originally one old building on this site before it was demolished to make two shops for the Co-op. In 1841 it housed John Velvin, upholsterer and cabinet maker, and Hannah Velvin, staymaker. Local directories show the whole space was occupied in 1886 by Edmund Long, Upholsterer, Cabinet Maker and Funeral Furnisher, storing his materials down at the Bull Pit. On the right side William Summers, Baker and Confectioner was in business here from 1899 to at least 1923, by which time H A Summers, possibly his son, had opened the Shambles Restaurant as a pastrycook and confectioner. The Summers were the same family as the blacksmiths up Market Street. In 1911 the shop was occupied by the London Central Meat Company (see photo on page 6).

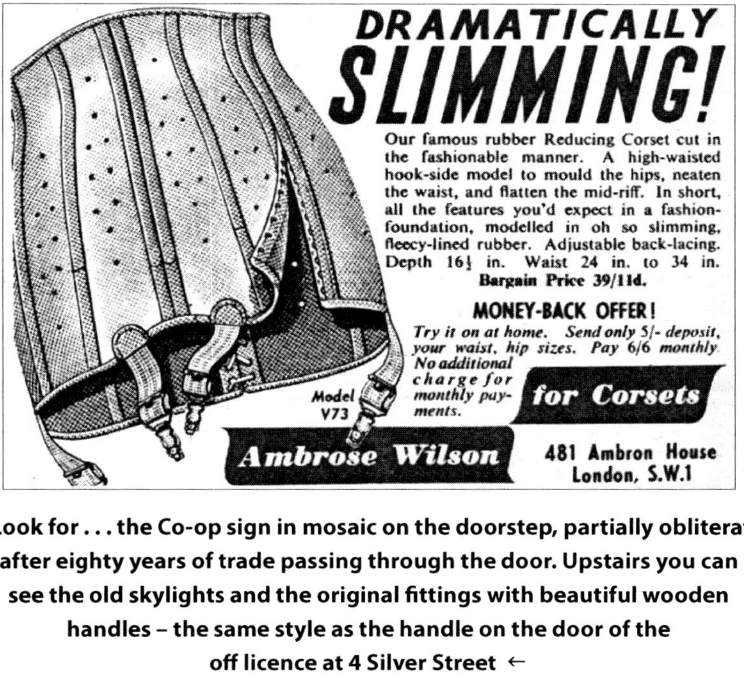

→ Look for . . . the Co-op sign in mosaic on the doorstep, partially obliterated after eighty years of trade passing through the door. Upstairs you can see the old skylights and the original fittings with beautiful wooden handles – the same style as the handle on the door of the off licence at 4 Silver Street ←

No. 3 Chisholm's Jewellers

In 1952 George Chisholm was continuing a long tradition of jewellers shops in these premises; a tradition which continues to this day.

Here was Mary Perry, milliner, in 1841, Joshua Deacon, watchmaker, in 1867, C Hart, jeweller and watchmaker in 1900 and Payne's in 1903, watchmaker, jeweller and purveyor of Spectacles and Eye Glasses.

No. 4 A Davis Grocers, Fishmongers

In 1952 this was a greengrocers and wet fish shop run by Charlie Davis, son of Albert Davis, a prominent figure in the town. He bought these premises in 1927 at an auction at the Swan Hotel for £850. In May 1928 the 'High Class Fish and Fruit Stores' was opened, with 'Fruit and Vegetables daily from the Davis's own gardens.' Albert Davis & Sons was a highly successful business, with another greengrocers shop in Market Street and two other shops in Trowbridge and Westbury in the 1950s. The family firm began in the 1860s with John Davis, a farmer in Bradford Leigh, who was listed as dairyman and greengrocer here from 1865 to 1869.

> *"Davis's window was open and the marble fish counter was exposed . . . the fish counter was on the left and on the right all the greengrocery. They used to serve you - you never helped yourself in those days. And old Charlie, if anyone was out the front in the Shambles and picked up an apple to have a look at it and put it down again, if he was serving you, he used to stop serving you and he'd go outside and polish that apple and put it back again!"* (CB12)

Albert Davis bought the shop from another grocers, the Couplands. Thomas Coupland started the business around 1895, when he was trading as Grocer and Patent Medicine Vendor. He was still there in 1911, using a handcart for deliveries. He handed it on to Ernest Coupland and, in 1923, Walter Coupland.

→ Look for . . . the Davis sign in mosaic tiles on the steps, the centre step now worn away by countless shoppers. The sign on the wall above the shop announces " A Davis, Fish, Fruit and Potato Merchants".
Inside the shop old paper advertisements are stuck to the wall – you can just about decipher "Tobacco" and "Baking Powder".
This wall shows clearly the line of the old sloping shelf in the window ←

No. 5 Misses Jackson, Fancy Shop

In 1952 the Misses Jackson sold gifts and wool to the ladies of Bradford on Avon at a time when knitting was the norm.

> *"We used to go and buy our wool there, and they would reserve it. People were not very well off in those days so they'd just go in and buy a ball or two of wool a week and do it that way."* (AB12)

At this time, wool was two shillings and threepence a ball (12p).

> *"It was a very dark shop, with this big tortoise stove throwing out heat in the winter.*

That's why it was nice to go in there. That was a big factor of our childhood, being warm! Everything was cold. The whole business of ice on the inside of the windows. It was colder then." (WS RS12)

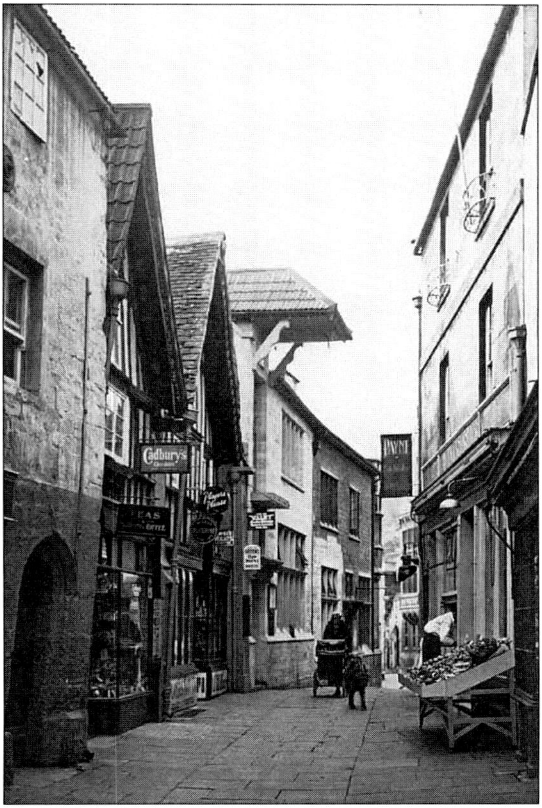

One older resident recalls the common practice of paying in instalments up to Christmas to help spread the load.

"Her window had toys in it and dolls, lovely dolls. I must have been about seven or eight I suppose and just before Christmas . . . there was this lovely doll in an orange dress and a little orange hat and I saw this doll and thought "Oh, what a lovely face she's got!" So my grandmother always came on a Friday and we were walking through the Shambles and i said "Oh, I do love that doll, grandma!"

And my mother said, "You've got enough dolls, you don't want any more now."

She had little black shoes on, I can see her now as plain as day. My grandmother said 'Well, if you're a good girl and I give you sixpence every Friday will you go and put it on the club card' because you could pay in sixpence a week and she said 'If you pay that in for that doll, when it comes to Christmas I will pay whatever is owing.' Oh, that made my day! So I went in every week and at Christmas my grandma paid for the outstanding bit. Oh, I was very lucky, I got that doll! She had a china face and the rest of the body was stuffed. She went everywhere!" (JS12)

In 1865 No. 5 was listed as William Butt, Grocer.

No. 6 Rawlings Florist

In 1952 Miss Young sold plants and flowers here in Karen's fruit and veg shop at the end of the Shambles. She lived around the corner in Coppice Hill and her father had a small nursery along Trowbridge Road, helping to provide her with produce.

Bradford Voices tells of an old lady who used to sell 'furmity' from this shop.[71] Furmity, or frumenty, was a nourishing porridge made from wheat, raisins, milk, eggs and syrup or rum. It could be pretty powerful. In Thomas Hardy's *The Mayor of Casterbridge* so much rum was added to the mix that one man ended up selling his wife at the market! Frumenty has been referred to as England's oldest dish and was particularly popular in the south-west. Country women in shawls and bonnets would come into Weston super Mare to sell small basins of frumenty on mid-Lent Sunday, and the tradition continues at Devizes on Mothering Sunday to this day. It seems to have disappeared from our diets by about 1880.[72]

In 1841 this was William Prior's grocer's shop but fifty years later was occupied by Mrs Rudman's China and Glass shop. *Kelly's Directory* shows her here in 1899 and 1911. She was most likely the widow of Cornelius Rudman who was here before her in 1887, listed as tailor and china dealer.

~ This little shop at the end of The Shambles marks the end of the Street Trail, an appropriate place to finish on the spot where Bradford's earliest market first began, around one thousand years ago ~

If you've enjoyed reading about the history of Bradford's shops, the bookshop in the Shambles has a good range of local interest books.

Many items from the old shops can be seen in the Bradford on Avon Museum above the Library, well worth the walk back over the bridge.

References and notes

1 Jones, Rev W H, *Bradford-on-Avon, A History and Description*, Wm Dotesio, The Library Press, 1907, p43 (Canon Jones was vicar of Holy Trinity Church from 1851 to 1885)

2 *Ibid*, p29

3 *Leland's Itin.*, ed. Toulmin Smith, i, 134-6, quoted in Jones, Rev W H, *Bradford-on-Avon, A History and Description*, Wm Dotesio, The Library Press, 1907, p167

4 Part of the Methuen Archives now at the Wilts Record Office WRO 1742/6786. Cited in Public Record Office, E179/234/193, quoted in *Wiltshire Archaeological and Natural History magazine*, Vol. 86, 1993

5 Fassnidge, Harold, *Bradford on Avon Past and Present*, Ex Libris Press, revised edition 2007, p32

6 Pigot's Directory, 1822-3, quoted in the *Victoria History of Wiltshire*, Vol. VII, ed. R B Pugh, Oxford University Press, 1953, p11

7 Langdon, Gee, *The Year of the Map*, Compton Russell, 1976, p12

8 *Kelly's Directory, Wiltshire*, 1907, quoted in *The Victoria History of Wiltshire*, Vol. VII, ed. R B Pugh, Oxford University Press, 1953

9 Fassnidge, Harold, *Ibid*, p167

10 Home Office correspondence. 52/2 H C Daubeny to Home Secretary, 2 April 1821, quoted in *The Victoria History of Wiltshire*, Vol. VII, ed. R B Pugh, Oxford University Press, 1953, p45

11 Fassnidge, Harold, *Ibid*, p145

12 The 1830 *Pigot Commercial Directory* lists seven butchers and six boot and shoemakers. By 1842 Pigot lists 12 butchers and 15 boot and shoemakers.

13 Langdon, Gee, *Ibid*, p43

14 A hot drink made from an infusion of herbs, usually salep or sassafras, with milk and sugar

15 A hackney coachman

16 Batchelor, Daniel, Reminiscences of Bradford 50 Years Ago by an Old Bradfordian in America. A Wiltshire Election 50 Years Ago. A letter from Daniel Batchelor of Utica, Oneida County, New York in the *North Wilts Mercury*, April 24, 1885 [Online], available: www.freshford.com/reminscences_of_bradford_on_avon.htm (24 February 2013)

17 Jones, Rev W H, *Ibid*, p68

18 *Ibid*, p68

19 Fassnidge, Harold, *Ibid*, p153

20 Dobson, Margaret, *Ibid*, pp56-64

21 Mock, J H, *Bradford on Avon and District, The War Years* (1939-1945), Makjok Publishing, 1997

22 http://www.statistics.gov.uk (7 May 2013)

23 http://www.massobs.org.uk (7 May 2013)

24 Mock, J H, *Ibid*

25 http://www.woolworthsmuseum.co.uk/1950s-firstselfservice.htm (3 March 2013)

26 Dobson, Margaret, *Ibid*, p195

27 Jones, Rev W H, *Ibid*, p66

28 Batchelor, Daniel, *Ibid*

29 Langdon, Gee, *Ibid*, p43

30 *Ibid*, p11

31 The Austin A40 Devon Road Test, *The Motor*, October 13, 1948

32 http://www.statistics.gov.uk (3 April 2013)

33 Thanks to Peter Leach for this

34 Dobson, Margaret, *Ibid*, p106

35 From a report by P M Slocombe, Wiltshire Buildings Record, 2000

36 Ponting, Kenneth, *Wool and Water*, Moonraker Press, 1975, p16

37 Thanks to Roger Clark, Curator of the Bradford on Avon Museum, for pointing this out

38 Dobson, Margaret, *Ibid*, p77

39 Jones, Rev W H, *Ibid*, p161

40 Fassnidge, Harold, *Ibid*, p167

41 Niblett, Bertram, *Memories of Bradford-on-Avon*, Wiltshire Library & Museum Service, 1981, p31

42 Howell, Jean, *Guardian Angel*, Bradford on Avon Preservation Trust. Harry Webley started as an apprentice in 1914 and retired 50 years later in 1964

43 Dobson, Margaret, *Ibid*, p236

44 Ashton, Mary, *Guardian Angel*, nos 63 & 64, Bradford on Avon Preservation Trust

45 Niblett, Bertram, *Ibid*, p25

46 Dobson, Margaret, *Ibid*, p208

47 Jones, Rev W H, *Ibid*, pp306-22

48 Niblett, Bertram, *Ibid*, p23

49 Dobson, Margaret, *Ibid*, p76

50 *Ibid*, p76

51 Niblett, Bertram, *Ibid*, p30

52 Harvey R and Harvey B, 'Bradford on Avon in the 14th century', *Wilts Archaeological and Natural History Magazine* Vol 86, 1993, pp118-29

53 Batchelor, Daniel, *Ibid*

54 http://www.wiltshire.gov.uk/bradford_on_avon_conservation_area_character_assessment_march_2008-2.pdf (17 April 2013)

55 Jones, Rev W H, ëA stroll through Bradford on Avon', *Wiltshire Archaeological & Natural History Magazine*, Vol 20, 1882, pp306-22

56 Langdon, Gee, *Ibid*, p14

57 Powell, W R, *Bradford on Avon, A History to 1950*, reprinted from the The *Victoria History of Wiltshire*, Vol VII, ed. R B Pugh, Oxford University Press, 1953, p46

58 Proposal approved by the Bradford on Avon Town Council, April 2013

59 Ashton, Mary, *Guardian Angel*, no 9, Bradford on Avon Preservation Trust

60 Langdon, Gee, *Ibid*, p45

61 http://www.federationoffishfriers.co.uk/pages/history--599.htm (17 April 2013)

62 http://www.bradfordonavonmuseum.co.uk (17 April 2013)

63 Dobson, Margaret, *Ibid*, p85

64 *Ibid*, p217

65 *Ibid*, p215

66 Jones, Rev W H, *Ibid*, p99

67 Fassnidge, Harold, *Ibid*, p163

68 *Colonel Polhill's Pukka Guide to Bradford on Avon*, Polhill Promotions, 1996, p13

69 Langdon, Gee, *Ibid*, p44

70 Niblett, Bertram, *Ibid*, p25

71 Dobson, Margaret, *Ibid*

72 White, Florence, *Good Things in England*, Jonathan Cape, 1832, reprinted Persephone, 1999

73 http://www.statistics.gov.uk (20 May 2013)

A Note on Prices

A straightforward calculation from pre-decimal currency to current values (one shilling equals 5p) is not a clear indication of a product's relative worth now as compared to the 1950s. Inflation has seen the "value" of £1 in 1952 increase to around £25 today. Or to look at it in reverse, something which costs £1 today would have been just 4p back then. Computing an accurate figure entails referring to the Retail Price Index and Gross Domestic Product figures for each year - or by assessing how long someone would have to work to buy the same product. The average wage in 1952 was £9 for men (for a 42 hour week)and £5 for women as compared to 2012 when the average wage was £495 for men (for a 32 hour week)and £318 for women.[73] However, I have not attempted to make any such calculations and hope that the simple calculation from sterling to decimal will suffice! The website http://www.measuringworth.com/uk is a useful resource.

Many thanks to the Bradford on Avon residents who have particularly contributed to this book with memories and photographs:

John Banks, Chris Bowyer, Audrey Broad, Roger Cooper, Andrew Jenkins, Vibeka Jenkins, Colin Johns, Roger Jones, Roger Mawby, Christian Penny, Wendy Street, Ralph Street, Joy Sully

Photo credits

Bradford on Avon Museum archives: 14, 19 (bottom), 30, 31, 34 (top), 35, 37 (top), 39, 41, 45, 46, 54, 55, 64, 65, 80, 81 (top), 82, 85 (top), 90, 96, 100 (right), 103

Wiltshire & Swindon History Centre archives: Front cover, 27, 29, 33, 44, 51, 52, 53, 61, 62, 66, 68, 69, 70, 74, 75, 78, 79, 86, 88, 89, 93, 95, 97, 102

Neil Mattingley: 2, 6, 13, 15, 16, 38, 40, 42, 43, 67, 73, 92, 99, 107

Christian Penny: 48, 49, 77, 85 (bottom), 104

Colin Johns: 34 (bottom)

Roger Jones: 36

Louise Gummer: 37 (bottom)

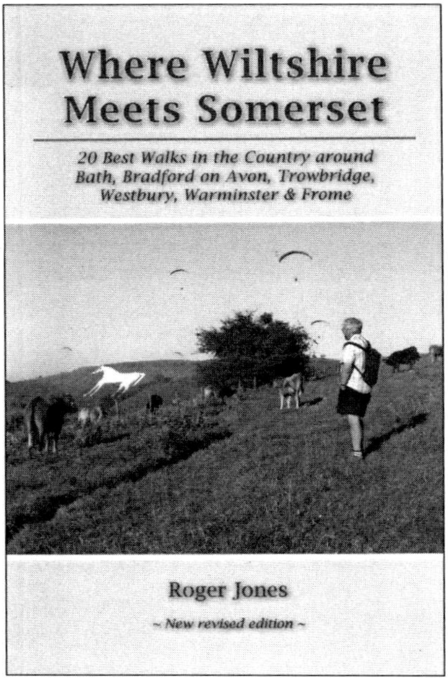

WHERE WILTSHIRE MEETS SOMERSET

20 best walks around Bath, Bradford on Avon, Trowbridge, Westbury, Warminster & Frome

by Roger Jones
128 pages
Illustrations & sketch maps
ISBN 978-1-906641-55-9
Price £7.95

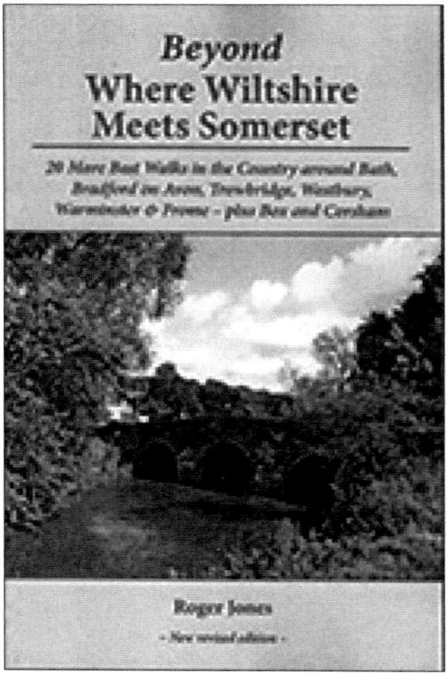

BEYOND WHERE WILTSHIRE MEETS SOMERSET

20 more best walks around Bath, Bradford on Avon, Trowbridge, Westbury, Warminster & Frome - plus Box and Corsham

by Roger Jones
128 pages
Illustrations & sketch maps
ISBN 978-1-906641-76-4
Price £7.95

Books from Ex Libris Press may be obtained via your local bookshop, from Amazon or direct from the publisher, post-free, using Paypal at

www.ex-librisbooks.co.uk

Please visit out website to view a complete list of our publications

EX LIBRIS PRESS, 11 Regents Place, Bradford on Avon, Wiltshire, BA15 1ED